A STORY OF LOVE

Beyond the
BLOOD

A STORY OF LOVE

MICHAEL CRAMER

Copyright © 2023 by Micheal Cramer

All rights reserved. No part of this book may be reproduced or used in any manner without written permission of the copyright owner except for the use of quotations in a book review.

For permission, contact the author via email@.com

First Published in the USA

ISBN:

DEDICATION

This is dedicated to my father, Patrice Cramer, who passed away from cancer, and my resilient Mom, Ashlee Cramer. My love for you two is boundless and ineffable.

TABLE OF CONTENTS

Preface 9
1. The Lockdown 11
2. The Diagnosis 16
3. Chemotherapy 33
4. The BMT 60
5. The First 100 Days 88
6. The Afterwards 98
7. Liver GVHD, Another Roadblock 109
8. The Great Depression 124
9. Healing 130
10. Love 140
Conclusion: My Message to You 170
Afterword 180

PREFACE

As we all know, life is full of struggles and hardships, but also beauty and hope. I have experienced both extremes in my short life. I have faced loss, pain, cancer, depression, and anxiety, but I have also gained life, love, and perspective from my family and my struggles.

As a teenager, I lost my father to cancer and watched my amazing mother struggle for years to keep us kids happy. Unfortunately, when things seemed to feel normal, and we were beginning to feel comfortable again, I was diagnosed with cancer. My Mom gave up her career to take care of me, and life has not been the same since. But it's not bad; we have found beauty in the pain and a beautiful purpose through all of this.

In this book, I share my story and journey of the last few years of my life. I also share the lessons I have learned and what I want you to take away from this reading in the final chapter. I hope you enjoy and take away a lot of important lessons from this.

I decided to publish my book to give you, the reader, a story of love and hope that will inspire you to live your life to the fullest every single day.

CHAPTER ONE

THE LOCKDOWN

It was March of 2020. The infamous Covid lockdown had begun. I was an 18-year-old college freshman, back home in Miami, feeling the blues of the quarantine. I was tired. I wanted to surf and work out, but the beaches and gyms were closed. Miami was a weird place to be during this time. Thousands had just come here for the spring break raves, and the Covid cases were skyrocketing.

I found myself spending most of my days skateboarding to the beach entrance and looking at the water from afar as the police officers glanced at me, making sure I knew that there was a fine line I could not cross to enter the actual beach itself. It felt wrong that the beaches were closed and everyone was just inside. The sun and water were supposed to heal, not harm. I would often find myself skating back home sad, questioning when this horrific lockdown would be over, and I would find myself back in the water, the gym, and school.

I had recently gotten my lifeguarding license and was about to have a job as a lifeguard, but that was on hold now. As a long-time surfer and windsurfer, the ocean was my home, and this job was something I was looking forward to.

March, April, and May dragged on. I fell into a slump. I was exhausted all the time. I had just gotten my heart broken. I liked this girl so much, but she dumped me as soon as the lockdown happened. I had no outlet to express myself except for home workouts and skating. I saw some friends sometimes, but I was paranoid about catching Covid. Most days, I kept to myself. I felt stuck in my head. I was so tired. I had night sweats. I felt worse and worse as the days went on. It felt like depression, but I wasn't sad. I just couldn't pinpoint it.

May 19th. It was my 19th birthday, and I invited a few of my "Covid-safe" friends over to celebrate. There was no going out or party, but we had some cake and parted ways.

As May came to an end, my friends and I found ourselves desperate for some surf. We heard news of a beach opening up in North Florida: New Smyrna Beach (NSB). We did not think twice; we booked the cheapest and closest Airbnb and drove 4 hours north to NSB. We surfed for three days straight and had the best time. I felt like myself again. My energy and happiness returned. It was a breath of fresh air. Catching amazing waves with my friends, getting out of Miami, and out of my head. I came back home rejuvenated and great. I did not feel that same sad feeling that came with my exhaustion.

But a few days later, I found myself coming down with a fever. I feared I had Covid. The fever lasted for a week, but it was mild and off and on. I didn't have a cough or flu-like symptoms. But I had a weird symptom: I was freezing after showering. I had to put the shower to extremely hot temperatures for my body to be satisfied, and my biggest challenge would be coming out of the shower. I would have to wrap myself in blankets and a jacket just to warm up post-shower. I was having all the symptoms of someone who is anemic. At least a quick Google search told me that. These days and nights of fevers, night sweats, and exhaustion pushed me to go see my family doctor and get some blood work done. My mom truly believed that I was anemic and that dark chocolate would help. I am not going to lie; it tasted good, but it did not help. My mom was vegetarian, and we ate a balanced diet growing up, so I doubted it was my diet. My brother, Steven, decided to accompany me to our family doctor's office. My doctor, Doctor Salinas, said I looked great and that she was not worried. She was going to have the results of my blood work in a few days. My brother and I drove home.

A few days later, I was driving to help my good friend, Juanchi, and his dad move to their new house. Juanchi and I grew up together sailing and windsurfing at our local yacht club. He had been a loyal friend of mine for years. As I was driving, I got a call from my Mom. She told me that Dr. Salinas called her and said we had to go to Nicklaus Children's hospital to meet a doctor. This doctor was a blood specialist, and because of Dr. Salinas's friendship with him, he was able to squeeze me in today on his busy schedule. I quickly turned around and drove home, and my mom and I drove together to Nicklaus Children's hospital.

We entered the doctor's office, signed in, and waited. The air felt weird. Something was off. I couldn't explain it, but I felt something was wrong. Maybe it was worse than being anemic or having Covid. I shut down those thoughts and looked around. It was strange to wait in a children's hospital office. I was 19, still a kid, but technically an adult.

After waiting for a bit, my name was called, and I was taken into a room with a nurse. She drew some blood and sent me to a waiting room. I waited for about 30 minutes. Then the results came back. The doctor, Dr. Dangulo, came in and talked to us. He looked serious. He wanted me to stay the night and do a bone marrow biopsy. I thought to myself, "Stay the night in the hospital? That's crazy." My mom and I agreed to come back the next day for the biopsy. On the drive home, I felt frustrated. This was going to be a hassle. What if I was anemic and needed blood transfusions all the time? I'm sure it's nothing. Why can't he just give me some iron pills and send me home? My thoughts raced, but I tried to calm them down.

We came back the next day at 7 am and went to the infusion center. I had to get a Covid test and then do this biopsy. I had never been under anesthesia before, so I was nervous. I also made the mistake of eating an apple before a procedure. Doctor Dangulo told me the previous day to be "NPO," but the term just flew over my head, and at the time, I did not know it meant no food or water after midnight. The nurse walked into my room, saw me eating the apple, and freaked out. She told me to stop eating it because I had to be NPO for the bone marrow biopsy. This small incident ended up delaying the biopsy by a long few hours. After my Covid test results came back, it had been a few hours, and it was time for my biopsy. A kind, tall male nurse named Andrew transported me to the minor procedure suite, and there I waited to be taken in for the bone marrow biopsy. On the way to the minor procedures suite, I asked the nurse named Andrew if he had ever been under anesthesia, and he said he had. He described it to me like once you get knocked out, the next thing you remember is waking up. This gave me some comfort, and I felt less nervous. Finally, it was time for my bone marrow biopsy. The nurses in the minor procedure suite started taking me to the operating room, and they began to infuse my IV with a medicine that they said would make me feel "drunk." After about 30 seconds, I was out.

CHAPTER TWO

THE DIAGNOSIS

"**W**hat you have is treatable. It's a form of leukemia/ lymphoma," that was the first thing the kind Doctor said when he walked into my recovery room. I was just waking up from a bone marrow biopsy. I was groggy, tired, out of it, and super confused. This was my first time ever under anesthesia, and when I woke up in this small, freezing, cold room, I was shocked. I felt like I was dreaming. I had come to the hospital thinking I was anemic; I had just been tired for a few months with some night sweats. I came here to get some bloodwork done and to find a solution to my low energy. Never in a million years did I expect this to happen. Never in a million years did I, Michael Cramer, an athlete my whole life, a newly trained gym rat and surfer, think that I would ever get diagnosed with cancer.

THE DIAGNOSIS

I sat in the room and looked at my mom. She looked uneasy but was holding her head up, trying to be strong so that I would not break down. She continued to talk to the doctor, and soon enough, the doctor began to ask me questions. "What do you like to do for fun?" he asked me.

"I love surfing," I told him.

He then nodded and smiled. I felt some relief and comfort knowing that my doctor was going to be someone who cared about me and my lifestyle. The doctor looked over at me and told me, "You have to do chemotherapy one way or another, and we need to admit you to the hospital right away." I agreed. I was fine with it.

On the hospital bed, with an IV in my arm, the nurses wheeled me around and put me in a gigantic elevator. We got off at the 6th floor: the oncology/hematology unit. On getting off the elevator, I looked around and felt scared. I saw a few bald kids with IV poles, looking weak, frail, sick, and hopeless. I was in shock and wondered, "Is this what's going to happen to me?" It couldn't be. I was a 19-year-old athlete, blond, handsome, tall, muscular, strong. I had never been hospitalized in my life. I felt like an alien, but I didn't know that this place would soon become my second home.

They put me in a room, and my mom and I checked it out. We thought, "This is not so bad." And the truth is, it was not bad at all. The room had a big TV, a couch, a chair, a nice bathroom, and a good view. It was better than I expected a hospital room to be. I had a room all to myself, which gave me a sense of relief. Hospitals are always a nasty place to be, but I felt better knowing my doctor was nice and that I had a big room all to myself.

It was around 4 p.m. on this devastating day when my mom decided to call my brother. I could hear my brother crying on the phone with my mom once he heard the news. My brother was at the gym when my mom called him, and he immediately left and rushed to the hospital. He came to see me, and so did my good friend, Alejandro, who was working out with him. My pediatrician, who had sent me to the hospital for the tests, also came to visit. For some reason, they let me have these three visitors despite Covid. The room had a good vibe, and I wasn't afraid to face cancer. It was a strange feeling. It felt like I had been preparing myself mentally and physically for this challenge in the last year, like it was something I had to overcome. The fact that my brother, my friend, and my pediatrician came to support me made me really happy.

But things changed when the visiting hours ended, and they had to leave, and it was just my mom and me. The doctor came in, sat next to me with a few nurses, and started to talk to me. "You can have a port or a PICC line," he said.

"A port or a PICC line? What is that?" I wondered.

The doctors and nurses explained that they are both lines used for chemotherapy and blood transfusions. The doctor was super kind and said, "So I know you are a surfer, which means the port will better suit you because it can get wet, and you can go in the ocean with it."

I asked him, "Can the PICC line get wet?"

He said, "No."

I said, "Then why have a PICC line if the port lets me do what I love?"

He said, "The PICC line can be placed here, but the port needs surgery. It goes under your skin near your chest."

I said, "I want the port so I can surf during my treatment."

He said, "Good idea. I'll try to get you into surgery tomorrow morning. We don't know your exact diagnosis yet, but we will soon. Then, we'll start your chemotherapy. For now, I'm giving you steroids. They help with all kinds of cancer."

I said, "Thank you so much." He left, and I started taking the pills called "Dexamethasone."

My first night sleeping in the Hospital was long, uncomfortable, and sleepless. As soon as morning came, the surgery team walked into my room. They told me they were going to take me to the OR and place my port, but first, they needed me to sign this form of consent. I signed the form of consent and was sent down to the waiting room to get prepped for the OR. I was tired, mainly exhausted from the amount of information I had to process and accept in the last 24 hours. I was honestly ready to be put to sleep by anesthesia, get the port placed in, and begin my treatment.

I was in my bed and wheeled to the Operating room. I looked up and saw a huge light right above me. It was just like the movies. Surgeons surrounded me, talking in what seemed like a foreign language. I tried to listen to understand what they were saying, but I couldn't understand a thing. The sound of the heart rate and blood pressure monitor I was hooked up to was too loud. One of the surgeons came up to me and said, "We are putting you on this table. Can you lift your legs for a second and get up on this table?" I did just that. Then I was placed on my side with a blue rubbery cushion on my head as I lay on his super hard bed in the middle of the operating room. The monitor beeped faster as my heart raced. "Beep, beep beep," the sound kept intensifying the more anxious and nervous I got.

"Take a few deep breaths," said one of the surgeons, "We are going to put this mask on you; all you have to do is breathe in and out for a few seconds, and you'll be out."

"Ok," I thought. The mask was placed on my face, and I began to breathe in and out. At first, I did not feel anything, and I was worried I was doing it wrong or there was a mistake, but a few seconds later, the room began to look funny, and my vision and hearing felt off. I was suddenly closing my eyes, feeling super groggy, and before I knew it, I was out.

I woke up in the recovery room, dizzy, confused, and in unbearable pain. The nurses were talking to me. I remember them asking me if I was okay. I was not okay. I was in so much pain, but the nurses were great, and they gave me pain medication to help. The next 30 minutes were a blur. The pain medication made me feel loopy, tired, and gross. The next thing I knew, I was back upstairs with my mom, in my room, unable to move my neck. I looked down, and all I could see were some fancy band-aids on my neck and chest where my port was inserted. I tried to turn

THE DIAGNOSIS

my neck and head so I could talk to my mom, but I couldn't. So I just spoke, and she came up to me and listened. She asked if I was okay. I told her I was in so much pain that I could not move. I could tell that she was shocked and sad for me. But we had no choice; we had to be okay and stay positive.

The rest of the day was rough. I was so hungry because of the new medication I had started (the steroid), and I was barely able to eat because of the pain that came from swallowing and moving at all. I was in severe pain the whole day. I was barely able to do anything. I couldn't move my neck, my throat was sore from the breathing tube they inserted during the surgery, and even talking hurt.

A few hours later, Alejandro came to visit me again. He greeted me as he entered the room, but I couldn't even turn my head to look him in the eyes. I appreciated his presence, but I felt like I really belonged in the hospital. I felt sorry for Alejandro, who just sat there while I lay in bed, sobbing from the excruciating pain.

Eventually, Alejandro left, and it was time for me to go to bed and get some much-needed rest. I called the nurse by using the small remote attached to the bed and clicking the "nurse" button to ask for pain medication. I needed to sleep. I was tired, hungry, and beat up from one surgery. How was I going to be able to beat cancer if a port insertion was so brutal to my body? Isn't chemotherapy one of the harshest things in the world for your body? I asked myself. I was scared, but I still felt like there was a reason this had happened. The nurse came into the room, and I glanced at her. She asked me what I needed, and I told her

I needed pain medication. She quickly returned with a syringe that had a piece of tape on it with some illegible writing. She disconnected the line that was giving me fluids from the pole (a pole is a big stand that holds the IV bag that delivers fluids or infusions) and injected the medication through my lines, directly into my port, and into my body. I felt the medication coursing through me, and suddenly, I felt numb all over. For the first time in what seemed like forever, I was pain-free, I could swallow, and I could relax. I was so tired that I fell asleep instantly.

 I woke up the next morning, and I felt optimistic. The next day was definitely better. I had my labs drawn that morning, which is when they take blood from your port or IV to check your blood counts. It turned out that I needed a blood transfusion. My hemoglobin was low. Hemoglobin is a protein in your red blood cells that carries oxygen. If you have low hemoglobin, you are likely to feel very tired and short of breath. I was a bit nervous to receive a blood transfusion, but it went well. It was strange to me at first, but I soon realized this would become my new normal. I looked at the pole next to my bed that was connected to my body through various lines, and I saw a red bag full of blood that was slowly dripping into my body through these lines. The lines were also red, showing the blood that was entering my body. The idea was odd to me. I was getting someone else's blood pumped into my body to make up for my low hemoglobin. I was not used to this. Just a few days ago, I was at the gym. Now, I had spent two days in the hospital, and I had no idea when I would go home. I ended up staying in the hospital for another six days. It was all a blur to me, and it went by so fast. I had constant visitors who were trying to figure out what kind of cancer I had. Every resident, nurse, and doctor who came into my room asked me a million questions that I couldn't answer and checked up on me. I became the hospital's mystery case. No one could figure out my diagnosis, and this was stressful. The days dragged on and on. I waited anxiously for some news about my treatment plan, but no one knew anything. I should have started chemotherapy by now, but all I was doing was taking Dexamethasone. I was terrified, and so was my mom, who stayed with me during this hospital ordeal. On the seventh day, the doctor came in and talked to us. He said he still didn't know my exact diagnosis, but he was going to send my results from the initial bone marrow biopsy to other hospitals around the country. He mentioned places like MD Anderson and other well-known cancer institutes in the U.S.

That day, he also sent me home. I did not feel ready to go home. I was so weak. They sent transport to get me from my room. They put me in a wheelchair. The guy who wheeled me out of the hospital was very nice. He was about 5'8", in his mid-20s, and had thin black hair. He wore a thick mask and goggles. He took me downstairs to the exit, and my mom went to get the car. It was my first time being outside in over a week. I was sweating so much. I could barely stand. I was so weak from spending only seven days in the hospital. Finally, after what felt like hours, my mom arrived with the car, and I stood up from the wheelchair to get into it. I stood up and felt like I was going to fall. I had lost all my muscle, strength, and stamina during this hospital stay. I opened the car door and basically fell into the seat. My face was red from the effort, and I felt my body trembling from the anxiety and fear that overwhelmed me when I realized how quickly I had deteriorated. My mom saw this and asked me if I was okay. I said, "No, I am not ok."

I cried in the car and felt nauseous the whole way home. Being in the car was like riding the world's most intense roller coaster. I clung to the seat, trying not to throw up at every turn, stop, and lane change that happened on the 30-minute drive home through Miami traffic. When we finally got home, I faced another challenge—getting from the car to the house. It was only about 20 feet, but there was grass and some stairs to climb. It was much harder than I remembered, and I barely made it inside. As soon as I got in the house, I walked to my mom's bed and fell asleep under the covers. I was exhausted from leaving the hospital and enduring the car ride. I passed out as soon as I got home.

I woke up the next morning confused, tired, and in pain. It was 9 am, and my mom had gone to work. I walked out of her room to get changed, and the first person I saw was my friend, Alejandro. He was sitting on my couch with Starbucks and some breakfast for me. I looked at him, laughed, smiled, and said hi, then quickly changed and sat down on the couch with him. I was still in pain from the port surgery and tired from the week spent in the Hospital. Alejandro seemed shocked at how bad and weak I looked, but he insisted we spend the day watching movies and being together. He was a real friend. He was there for me when I needed him the most. I love this guy, I thought to myself, and boy, was I happy to see him. We spent the whole day watching Tarantino movies and eating food. I was super hungry. The steroids I was on had that effect, I learned. Every bite of food tasted amazing. We munched on chocolate croissants from Starbucks and cashews all morning.

Later in the day, Alejandro left and went back home. My mom came home, and we just relaxed for the rest of the day. I had nearly forgotten about everything that I had gone through in the Hospital the last week because of my time with Alejandro. But quickly, my mom and my body reminded me. My mom had received a call from my doctor, and I had hoped it was a call that said they knew what my diagnosis was. To my dismay, it wasn't. He called to ask how I was doing and said they would know my exact diagnosis in about two weeks. "Two weeks?!" I said to my mom, "Are you kidding me?! These are going to be the longest two weeks of my life!"

And you could bet your bottom dollar that those were the longest two weeks ever. It was painful, living with the anxiety, knowing that I was going to be home for the next two weeks before figuring out my diagnosis. What if I am delaying my treatment and getting worse because they cannot figure out what I have?! I kept wondering. My mom and I were glued to our phones, waiting for the doctor to text to see if anything came up sooner or if he somehow knew the diagnosis before the 2-week period. And so the days went by.

On July 22nd, 2020, a few days after being home. I decided to try to work out to pass some time. But this workout was not the same one I did just weeks ago. A few weeks ago, I was in the gym lifting 225 pounds and bench pressing 145 pounds for repetition. This work out I was doing at home was me curling a can of soup, and I was struggling immensely. It was unreal how much strength I had lost in such a short period of time. I struggled to lift these cans of food and felt out of breath with every set and repetition performed. I was working out with my mom; she was the one who was helping me attempt to get stronger. But it was so difficult, and it made me sad because I knew it would only get more difficult from here on. I knew that chemotherapy would not be nice to me at all. But that did not stop me. I did not give in to my weakness and mental struggles. I believed that I would gain enough strength back before I figured out my diagnosis so that I would be strong enough to face cancer and defeat this disease that had taken my father away from me years ago. It was personal to me. It was all so traumatizing as well. I lost my father to cancer, specifically lymphoma, and the doctors were telling me I might have lymphoma. I knew I needed to be strong to get through this.

A few days later, we received a text from my doctor. I was so excited, and I thought it would be about the diagnosis, but instead, he asked us to come to the Hospital for some blood work and a meeting. We went to the Hospital the next day. I was sitting in the waiting room with my mom, waiting for my name to be called so that I could get my blood pressure, height, weight, and blood work done. It was freezing cold in the waiting room and just cold in the hospital in general. However, for some reason, I was not cold. My armpits were sweating, and I could feel the anxiety start to creep over me as my name was finally called. The nice lady taking my vital signs sat me in a chair in a small room right outside the doctor's office. The room was full of kids' stickers, pictures of little kids bald from chemotherapy, and signs of hope everywhere. Yes, I am definitely being treated in a children's hospital, I thought to myself. It was comforting because the nurse taking my vitals was so kind. She asked me if I was okay after she took my vitals, and I asked why. My blood pressure was through the roof; it was about 140/100. I was nervous, and she could tell. I took a deep breath and stayed as calm as possible when she retook my vitals. Beep. Beep…. Beep…….. Beep. My heart rate and blood pressure finally dropped to normal levels after I calmed down. The nurse looked at me, smiled, and told me it was time for her to draw some labs. She told me she was going to do a finger prick. She reached into her drawer full of needles, bandaids, and all the medical supplies one can dream of and came out with a small white and blue finger stick that was going to be used to take my blood. She pricked my finger with it and then applied pressure to my finger, squeezing blood out of the tip into vials and filling them with as much blood as possible. I didn't even know that much blood could come out of one small finger tip. It was shocking to see. She kept putting pressure on my finger to release all the blood she could into these vials. After a few minutes of filling vials with my blood, we were finished. The nurse sent me to a room to wait for the doctor.

The room was a typical doctor visit type of room. It had a bed with a long white sheet of paper on it, a few chairs to the side, a computer, and signs about health warnings all over the wall. My mom and I waited in this room for about 30 minutes for the doctor and for the lab results to be ready so that we could discuss my labs with the doctor to see if I was okay. The doctor walked in with a smile on his face and a few papers in his hand. He asked me how I was doing, and he was very content to see that I was doing okay and looked better. He explained that my lab results had improved a bit and that this was good because it meant the steroids he had started on me and that I was still taking were useful and effective to my body. But immediately after he said this, his smile disappeared, and he asked me to follow him to his office.

His office was nice. It was big, full of chairs, a table, and a drawing board. There was also a shirt that read, "Fighting cancer, now that's a full-time job." He sat me down in a chair, and with his nurse practitioner in the room, they began to explain things about cancer to me. It started to feel like one of those moments in the movies where someone hears from a doctor that they don't have much time to live. It was like everything went blank to me for a second, and I started to cry. The doctor was giving me the "you have cancer talk." It suddenly became so real and scary. The doctor used the drawing board to explain how I possibly got cancer. He explained that because I had mono one year ago, this could be a link. His theory was that when I had mono, my body was fighting an infection. Then, when the mono went away, my body never stopped fighting this infection, making my cells replicate and replicate, causing cancerous cells to be brought into my body. Really?! MONO?! A kissing disease that I had last year in highschool was going to be the reason I had to go through cancer treatment?! I asked myself. I was shocked and felt like this was impossible. How did this happen to me? How was I sitting in a room getting a "you have cancer talk" at the age of 19 when, just a few months ago, I was in college living a normal, healthy life? I was shocked, and then the Doctor (his name is Dr. Dangulo) went on. He explained to me that cancer does not equal death. He could tell that I was worried about that. He knew the history of my father passing away from cancer because I told him about it. But Doctor D was sure that these two cancers were not related. He was positive that it had nothing to do with any of the genes passed down.

In a way, that was a relief. I was still shocked, but it gave me some hope that I would be okay. Dr. D told me to come back to the hospital in a week and that they would most likely have my diagnosis by then. Right now, he was eliminating possible diagnoses and wiring it down to a few that it could be. He said he would know the exact diagnosis in about a week. I went home that day even more anxious than I was before. I was scared that Dr. D even said, "Cancer does not equal death," because, for some reason, I was not thinking about death at all, but when he brought that up, it really made me question if I would end up beating this mysterious disease.

The next week was long, dreadful, and full of anxiety. But it finally passed, and on Friday, July 31, we got a call from Dr. D telling us to come in on Monday, August 3rd, and be prepared to stay for a few days. He knew the diagnosis but didn't want to tell us until he saw us on Monday. I was scared. Was he hiding something from us? Was it a diagnosis so bad that he did not want us to know what it was until he saw us? I tried hard all weekend to shut my thoughts out, but it was impossible. I was anxious and afraid of what was to come on Monday.

The weekend dragged on, but finally, Monday came. We packed a suitcase filled with clothes, ready for the hospital stay. It was a humid early Miami morning on August 3rd of 2020 when we left our house in our white Volvo and took off to go to Nicklaus Children's Hospital. I played music in the car. I played Jack Johnson, which is very calming music that made me happy. But something just felt off; something felt weird on the drive there. Something I could not explain. It just felt like the day was going to be intense. We had waited for what felt like years for this day to come. It was finally here, and we were finally going to figure out my diagnosis and get on the path to treatment. Yet it just felt weird.

We arrived at the hospital. I was wearing my favorite shoes, a silver chain around my neck, and a nice black T-shirt. We parked the car in the garage, walked down the stairs to the first floor, and made our way towards the oncology office. On the way to the office, I saw a sign I had never seen before. It read "Bone Marrow Transplant". Hmmm, I thought to myself. Isn't this what my Dad needed to get to survive his cancer, but he never made it to? Yes. It was.

THE DIAGNOSIS

We walked into the office, checked in, and sat down on the small but comfortable chairs that we had become accustomed to. While waiting, my mom and I played a game called 2048 on our phones and challenged each other to see who was going to win first. But neither of us got that far before I heard the words "Michael Cramer" and saw Dr. D open the door. He greeted us with a half smile and a nod, and then he brought us to one of the small patient rooms in his Clinic. He sat us down. This was the moment we had been waiting for for weeks. I was finally going to find out my diagnosis. It was freezing cold in the room, but sweat still dripped down my shirt and armpits as I anticipated the words that would come out of his mouth in the next few minutes.

"Hepatosplenic T-Cell Lymphoma," he said. This was a mouthful to me, and I had no idea what it meant. I just knew it was a form of lymphoma, and the only connection my mind made was the fact that my father died of lymphoma.

"You have to do 2-6 cycles of chemotherapy to get into remission, and then you need a bone marrow transplant," Dr. D said.

"A bone marrow transplant," I thought. This was the procedure my dad needed to get in order to live. But he never got it. He was too sick, and he passed away. It was like this whole cancer thing was a redemption. I felt like all of this had been passed down to me so that I could suffer but beat this and show my dad, who is in heaven, that I did it for him. Dr. D explained that I needed to be admitted to the hospital immediately and taken to my room in the 6th tower as soon as possible. I was starting my first round of chemotherapy that day, and I was told I would be staying in the hospital for the next five days. Well, here goes nothing, I thought, as I took a deep breath in and began walking to the elevator that would take me up to the 6th tower, where my new life and journey would begin.

CHAPTER THREE

CHEMOTHERAPY

I t started off slow. It was a hot summer day, and when I arrived at the 6th tower this time, I knew it was the real deal. Today, I would start chemotherapy. My life will never be the same, but I felt ready. I felt like I had been waiting for this moment for a long time. Those two weeks had been painful, full of anxiety, and stressful. But now it was time.

I got into my room with my mom and looked around. This was going to be my home for the next five days. The room was nice. It had a view of the hospital's garage, but this view was also right where the sun set every evening. The room had a nice bed for me, although a little small for my liking because I was 6'1 and 19 years old in a children's hospital. Right in front of my bed was a nice

TV on the wall next to the bathroom. The bathroom was small and had a tiny chair in it to sit down in the shower in case you were too tired to stand. It was a nice room to be stuck in for five days, I thought to myself.

The nurse finally came into the room with a table. It was time for her to access my port so that I could start my chemotherapy right away. The table had a huge blue cloth on it and had sealed bags full of syringes, vials, and a 1-inch needle. It was time to access my port. I was a little nervous, not going to lie. The nurse lifted my shirt to the side and had me take out my arm through the right sleeve so that my shirt was only on my left side. She did this because my port was on the right side, and she needed space to clean the area before she could access it. She cleaned the area around my chest with a white stick with a circular ending. After she cleaned the area, it was time to stick the 1-inch needle into my port through my skin. I was nervous and almost sweating. She counted 1…2….3… and then she did it. She stuck the needle into my port through my skin. I honestly did not feel anything but a little push. I thought it would hurt way more than it did. Now that my port was accessed, I was hooked up to an IV pole and waited for the chemotherapy to arrive.

This took a long time, but finally at the end of the day, at around 10 p.m., it arrived. The night nurse hung the bag of chemo on my pole and started it. Finally, I thought. I stayed up late that night watching basketball on the T.V. until I fell asleep while a disgusting bright yellow bag of toxins and chemotherapy was being infused into my body.

CHEMOTHERAPY

The next day was when it all really hit. I was sitting in bed and had the sudden urge to go to the bathroom. I was on Facetime with my friends. I was catching up with them and giving them a full update on what was going on. At around the middle of the call, I told them I had to get up. I walked to the bathroom with my pole and pulled my pants down to urinate. As soon as I started urinating, I began to scream. I had a pain so sharp in my back that I could not bend over without feeling like I was going to pass out. I had to pee so badly, but I was in so much pain. My mom heard me scream and immediately called the nurse to see what was going on. It turns out the nurse gave me a medication called "Lasix," which makes you pee. And sometimes, it can really hurt. I spent the rest of the night in my bed, peeing into a urinal and cringing in pain every time I had to go. And boy, let me tell you, I had to go A LOT. Lasix made it feel like you were peeing every ounce of fluid out of your body. It sucked.

The next few days were fortunately way better than that night. My brother came to visit every day. When I had the energy, we would walk around the 6th tower unit, taking laps, talking, and laughing. It felt good to see him. He represented something normal. I missed normal; the last few days had been everything but normal to me.

One such day, after our walk, my brother left, and Doctor D. came to check on me. He came into the room with a stack of papers and an excited look on his face. He explained to my mom and me that he found this new medication that had been proven to help with this type of cancer that I had. It was not in the original regimen, but my doctor said it was cutting-edge. He was inspired and wanted to do everything he could to make me better. This new medication was called "Peg". It would cost me an extra day in the Hospital to receive this chemotherapy, but I was totally down for it if it meant a chance at a sooner remission. If it was something that could save my life, I was up for it.

The next day came, and it was time to receive this "Peg." I was nervous because this medication could cause adverse reactions, and that scared the crap out of me. My Nurse could tell that I was anxious to receive this. She was an angel, though. She stayed with me in my room and talked to me the whole time while I received this medication. She was beautiful, smart and funny. We had a long conversation about how I love surfing, the ocean, and everything to do with water. This nurse was the opposite. She was afraid of the beach because of the sharks, and I teased her about this. Thankfully, I did not react to the medication and was fine. I finished the medication a few hours later with no adverse reactions, and I was so happy.

After five long days in the hospital, it was time to go home. It had been an adventure, for sure. I knew there was so much ahead of me, but after completing the first five days, it all seemed more possible. Before we left the hospital, the head nurse coordinator of the 6th tower had some instructions for us before I was discharged. I was to be sent home on lots of medications. She gave us a full paper and sat my mom and me down for about 2 hours, explaining everything I was taking, the possible side effects, everything that could happen, and when to come to the hospital if an emergency happened. Boy, was I scared. Nausea, vomiting, diarrhea, hemorrhoids, hair loss, loss of appetite, insomnia, and more. These were the most common side effects of everything I was taking. I had not felt many side effects at that point, but I knew that would all change soon. I was scared, but in a way, ready. The five days in the hospital were long, but honestly, it was not that bad.

Going home was a miracle. I was free and not hooked up to a machine, which meant I did not have to shower with an IV pole attached to me. I felt so good. I could eat food from home, and not that disgusting hospital food that I really do not think even counts as food. As soon as I got home, I took a nice shower, looked at myself in the mirror, and realized I looked a little bit like the Michelin Man. I was bloated, full of fluids, and weighed 170 pounds. I went to bed that night, and I swear I got up at least ten times to pee. I woke up the next morning and weighed 157 pounds. Over one night, I lost 13 pounds. That's how full of fluids I was, with just one hospital stay.

I was so nervous about the side effects of chemo that I had heard about: the weight loss, the hair loss, the loss of appetite, the nausea, and the first five days I spent in the hospital felt like a breeze. I was mainly tired and just had anxiety about what was going to happen. But when I got home, it all hit me: I got these terrible mouth sores, everything was coming, and I was feeling all the side effects right away. Immediately, I was losing my hair. It was falling out in the shower, in my bed, and everywhere I went. I sat down before I took a shower and put my hands through my hair to fix it and play with it like I always do. I brought my hand down from my head, and there it was, strings of hair, literally all over my hand. This was it. My hair was going to be gone. I was really going to become a bald cancer patient. It was emotional. Running my hands through my hair and feeling it come out in clumps gave me a feeling of mortality. I felt that cancer had finally hit me. I was losing my hair, I felt weak, and I had mouth sores. I felt like an alien. I realized that I was not a young, healthy kid anymore. I had cancer.

I soon learned the specific cancer I had had no protocol. I learned that Hepato Splenic Lymphoma was rare, aggressive, and did not have a high survival rate. Still, I refused to google it because I did not want to put anything else in my head. I realized that was why this round of chemo had hit me so hard. It was because I was doing one of the most intense chemotherapy regimens.

As soon as my hair began to fall out in clumps, I realized it was time to shave my head. It was a hot summer day, and my mom, brother, and I walked over to the barber across the street from our house. My brother had vowed to shave his head along with me to show his full support. We walked into the barber shop, and I saw Dan, the guy who had cut my hair for years and years. I knew I looked different; my face was puffy from steroids, my hair was a mess, super thin at this point, and all curled up in different ways. Dan was so happy to see us, though. He had a huge smile on his face and was grateful to see that I was ok for the time being.

He sat me down in a chair and began to shave my head. I looked at myself in the mirror the whole time. Slowly, all my beautiful blonde, curly, wavy, and thick hair was coming out, falling to the floor in clumps, never to be seen again in the same texture. I looked in the mirror, and it was all so surreal. I was bald. There was not much of a hairline left, and I could barely recognize myself besides my thick brown eyelashes and jawline that was barely visible because of the steroids that made my face puffy. Although my brother, my mom, and Dan looked at me when I was finally all shaved and said I looked amazing, I knew they were trying to comfort me, but it worked.

Now, it was time for my brother to shave his head. He was so excited that he could barely hold in his excitement. My brother is a huge gym rat with lots of muscle, so I am sure he was pretty excited to see what he looked like bald and good. His blue eyes, tight jawline, and perfect hairline made him look even more like a model. He looked like a bald, strong lifter. He looked at me and smiled. He was so happy to have done this for me, and I could tell. He came up next to me, and we took a photo together in Dan's hair salon. Both of us stood tall at 6'1, bald and smiling. You could tell in the photo that I was the sick one, though. My brother's muscle, posture, and energy just showed it all in that photo. We tried to pay Dan for his service, but he said it was his treat and that he just wanted to do everything he could to help our family. He is a great guy. We left the salon and walked home. As soon as I got home, I checked my phone and saw a few videos sent to me by my friends. They were all shaving their heads for me. I felt so happy, I wanted to cry. Geronimo, Maximo, Juanchi, Nicky, and Alejandro came over after I saw this video, and we all looked at each other's bald heads. We laughed, took pictures, and even made a video of us walking out the front door of my house one by one with "The Rocky theme song" playing as we all flexed our bald heads and looked straight at the camera, smiling. I was so happy. My friends were so real to me. They supported me so much and really loved me. The whole time they were there that day, we all just made fun of how dumb and funny we all looked. It was fun. It was fun to laugh and joke about something that serious. I felt motivated and hopeful about my future. I even decided that I would try to stay as active as possible during this intense treatment and try to stay in school. I was mentally strong, and I was an athlete. I really believed that I could do it, but it was not that easy.

The next day, I had to go to the hospital to get platelets and do a bone marrow biopsy to see the progress I was making during treatment and to see how much cancer was still in my blood. I was in the infusion unit at around 8 am that morning. I would have my first Zoom class later that day at 1 pm. I went to the minor procedures suite and was ready to go under general anesthesia for my bone marrow biopsy when my mom and I unexpectedly met a wonderful family.

Between the small curtains separating the waiting areas in the minor procedure suite, we started a conversation with the other family. Their young son was also a cancer patient, and his father chatted with my mom. His parents were both trying to cope with their child's illness and maintain some normalcy. My mom and I joined the conversation, telling them about my recent diagnosis and my upcoming class. They praised my determination to continue my education despite my treatment, saying it was a good way to distract myself from cancer. We said goodbye to this family when it was time for my procedure.

I went to sleep under general anesthesia for my bone marrow biopsy and woke up in the recovery room. "CLASS!" I yelled out as soon as I gained consciousness back from being super groggy. We hurried home, leaving the hospital behind. I was drained from the morning's tests and infusions, but I managed to grab my laptop, pen, and notebook. I opened the zoom link sent to me by my professor and joined the zoom. Everyone had their own camera's on. Everyone in the class had their cameras on, showing their healthy, alert faces and their full heads of hair.

I didn't even have the confidence to put my camera on and show everyone my bald head. I took notes vigorously the whole time and was exhausted by the end of the class. I did not grasp any of the material. I felt like a failure. I was so exhausted from chemotherapy's side effects, lack of sleep, and everything else that had gone on that day that I began to sob. Tears began to flow out of my eyes like a river, and a huge frown settled on my face. I grabbed my pillow and cried into it for minutes. I then called my mom, who was at the store and said, "Mom, I have cancer. It's really happening. I can't do this. I can't do school. I'm too exhausted, angry, sad, and scared. I need a break. I'm sorry."

She rushed back home and comforted me on my bed. "I have cancer, Mom. This is not real. I can't do this. I'm sorry." I sobbed. I was having a huge mental breakdown. I was screaming and balling tears. It was like everything had hit me that day. It was like cancer had become real all of a sudden, and I just felt so overwhelmed. I was so scared. I cried and cried until she eventually calmed me down.

This was a huge moment of realization for me about what I was really facing—the possibility of death. Another huge moment that hit me was during my first chemotherapy admission. Some social workers came to my room and asked me about Make a Wish. Make a Wish? I wondered. How did I go from surfing in New Smyrna Beach three weeks ago to being a dying kid? I didn't know much about Make a Wish, but I thought it was for people who had no hope. I was terrified. Were they hiding something from me? Did they think I was not going to make it? Was that why they wanted me to make a wish? I cried to my mom. "Am I really a Make-a-Wish kid?"

She said, "No, honey, you are going to be fine. They do this for every patient, and you don't even qualify because you are 19. They do this for kids 18 and under." I was still stunned. I had just started chemotherapy, I had just been diagnosed with a cancer I couldn't even pronounce, but I knew it was a type of lymphoma, and my dad died of lymphoma. I was living in a hospital with a port in my chest, not sleeping, feeling exhausted, eating horrible food, and fighting cancer. My world was upside down. Cancer, chemotherapy, and Make a Wish—these were things I had only heard of or seen on TV. But they had become my reality. I realized then that I had to be strong. I had to do everything I could to beat this disease. I wanted to do it for my father. I felt like if I could survive this, I could honor his memory and have a special bond with him now that he is resting in heaven.

While I was home from treatment, I stayed active and kept up with my friends. I worked out as much as I could, even if that meant curling and lifting cans of soup in my room. I wanted to be strong physically because I knew every round of chemo would just knock me down again. And that was how it worked, in fact. By the end of my first 21-day cycle, I was feeling pretty good again. I was able to walk, my mouth sores had gone away, and I was feeling a little bit stronger.

The good thing about having a port was that I was allowed to get it wet. I could go into the ocean when I had the proper blood counts for it. So, towards the end of my last cycle of chemotherapy, I went into the ocean. It was when I was finally feeling better again. It was the first time I had gone in the water since being diagnosed with cancer. I was at a public beach. My face was full of acne from steroids, I was bald, had no muscles, and was pale as a ghost. People at the beach were looking at me. I could feel it, but I just did not care. I felt so happy to be alive and at the beach that it did not bother me. I felt the ocean water on my body, and it was so healing—mentally and physically. It felt amazing to not be thinking about cancer or worried about my blood counts but to just be in the moment. It felt like the happiest moment of my life. I was so grateful to be allowed in the ocean. I wasn't even worried if people were looking at me. I was full of scars on my back, and I embraced it. I used to go to the beach when I was healthy and worry if people were judging me, if my muscles weren't good enough, or if I had some acne when, in reality, I looked great. But here I was, a full-blown cancer patient, a port in the chest, scars all over, and a bald head. Yet, I did not care what I looked like. It did not matter to me. I was just happy to be at the beach. It felt like the best day ever.

That beautiful evening at the beach ended, and it was time to be admitted to the hospital again and start my second round of chemotherapy. I knew it was going to be more difficult, have more side effects, and knock me down again. I had to stay the first five days of my 21-day cycle in the hospital receiving chemotherapy. This time around, I really fit in. I was bald, pale, skinny, and frail. I would walk the halls and see other patients, and they did not look alien-like to me anymore. They looked like my family. They looked like me. They looked like people going through a tough time who needed extra support, just like I did.

I had lots of support. I decided to post about what I was going through on Instagram to let the people who cared about me know what was happening. The support was great, but some messages scared me. Not everyone was as positive as I was. People messaged me, and I could tell they were really scared for me. I had people tell me how sorry they were for me, and it felt like some people were messaging me, thinking I was dying, which scared me even more. Still, there were people who sent me wonderful messages—people who messaged me inspiring stories about how someone in their family had gone through cancer, and they are fine now. I had people message me wishing me a smooth recovery and telling me I got this. I was really encouraged by these messages, and they motivated me to push myself, stay positive, stay active, and try to be myself as much as I could even though I was stripped down to nothing, receiving chemo in a hospital bed. However, I truly believed this was meant to happen to me, that it was not a coincidence, that this was my path for some reason, and although it is not a path anyone would choose, it was given to me.

I remember when I had finally completed my third 21-day cycle of chemotherapy and was finally in remission. I had become accustomed to the hospital at this point, and it was my norm. I was supposed to be heading into the hospital for my Bone marrow transplant as early as October 12th.

The day was September 28th of 2020. I went to the hospital and got a CBC done. I met with a lady named Jennifer, who was the head of the Bone marrow transplant clinic. She gave me some good news and bad news. We figured out that my brother and sister were not 100% matches for my transplant. My brother was a 50% match, and my sister was not a match at all. Fortunately, there had been some people from a registry called "Be the match" who were a match for my bone marrow.

That day, when I returned from the hospital, I decided to nap. I fell asleep and had a horrible dream. In this dream, I stood up and looked in the mirror. My head was full of hair, my eyebrows were thick, and I looked really healthy. I soon realized this was not normal. I screamed in my dream, and when I looked back into the mirror, all my hair was gone, like it had just fallen off. I woke up gasping for air. I was terrified and stressed. I was about to undergo a bone marrow transplant, and I had to do radiation therapy first. I knew I had to go to a different hospital to do radiation before my transplant, and this was freaking me out. The thought of being alone in a room, receiving radiation for more than half an hour a day, filled me with anxiety. It seemed unreal. I needed the radiation to wipe out the cancer and my bone marrow so that I could get a transplant and a new, healthy immune system. But it sounded so scary to me.

 I remember October 1st very well. It was the day of my BMT work-up. I had to undergo a lot of tests to prepare me for the transplant. I had a complete blood count, an EKG, an echo, a pulmonary function test, and countless other labs. The work up for a bone marrow transplant is pretty extensive. I remember being so excited about this. I felt so ready to have my transplant and begin the road to recovery that every day closer to my admission made me happy.

 The bone marrow transplant was not going to be easy, though. I would have to spend four to six weeks in the hospital, without visitors, confined to my room, and isolated from everyone. I would be at a high risk of infection for months, and I would have to be very careful. I was told that I could not go to the ocean or hang

CHEMOTHERAPY

out with my friends until a year after the transplant. I was also not allowed to be in the sun at all. It was real. It was scary. And it was my future.

But I was also grateful to have a chance to live and beat this disease. I did not let it bother me too much. The only thing that haunted me was the radiation. I could not get it out of my head. I would have to be transported every day to a different hospital at 5 a.m. in an ambulance and spend the whole day there, getting radiation twice a day. I just had to endure the radiation. The rest would be easy, right? I had already gone through three rounds of chemotherapy, and I had survived. I only had mouth sores, nausea, vomiting, and a bald head. It could not be worse than that, right? After the transplant, I would be done with treatment, and in a year, I would be surfing again!

The reason that I had to get a bone marrow transplant was because the cancer I had was known for coming back after treatment had finished. The transplant would give me a new system of blood and, hopefully, a cancer-free one. It would increase my chances of long-term remission.

I was also in a pretty good mood because when I went to the hospital that day, I met a kid who had a bone marrow transplant about a year ago. He was doing very well, and although he was a lot younger than me, he told me the hardest thing was going to be eating because your appetite and stomach changes a lot during a transplant. That day, I also met with the other head of the BMT Clinic. Her name was Maylin. She explained everything she could.

She told me that being positive and active was going to help me a lot and that I was going to be taking about 20 pills a day after my transplant for a while. This freaked me out. I hated pills and could only imagine why I would be taking so many medications. But it was the BMT doctor who explained the transplant the best to me.

A few weeks ago, during my second round of chemotherapy, the BMT doctor, Doctor Galvez, walked into my room and sat down. He talked to my mom and me for over an hour, and we bonded over movies. We loved movies from Star Wars all the way to Frozen. He was a super nice guy who loved to talk. He wore goggles, a giant face mask, and green scrubs. He was about 5'9 and had slick black hair. Dr. Galvez was a guy I knew I would get to know very well in the future. He explained the bone marrow transplant to me like it was a seed. He said that they were wiping out my old bone marrow with chemotherapy and radiation and then planting a new seed in me with this new bone marrow. The whole idea of this new seed was that, at first, it is nothing; it has no immunity, no strength, and it has not grown yet. They would use immuno-suppressive medications to make sure my body does not reject the bone marrow, and slowly, over time, they would take away these medications and let my new bone marrow become my new immune system and grow into this flower, slowly. It was a beautiful analogy because, at first, your immune system is very weak. It is a baby flower, but with time, this marrow grows stronger, taller, and becomes a full-on beautiful flower. Dr. Galvez, Maylin, and Jennifer all showed me that there was hope, and knowing that

CHEMOTHERAPY

they were going to be my doctors and be with me on the next step of my journey really encouraged me. They were wonderful people and were very nice to me.

The transplant process was complicated. I needed radiation as well as chemotherapy, and it was time to meet with the radiologist at Baptist Hospital. I had to go in for a simulation of radiation to understand what I was getting myself into and also to meet the doctor who would be administering my treatments while I was radiation at Baptist to prepare me for my bone marrow transplant. The day was October 2nd, and I arrived at Baptist at around 8 am. I had to do a Covid test before I could meet with the doctor and do my simulation. This hospital was different from the children's hospital I was used to. Baptist was gigantic, the walls were at least 30 feet high, and everything was high-tech. It felt far too futuristic to be a hospital. I had to wait in a small chair by a window to get my covid test done. It was done in a tent, and I waited for my results to come back so that I could meet with the doctor and do this simulation. The test finally came back negative after over an hour of waiting, and now it was time to walk down the hallway and find this doctor—Doctor Hall, the doctor who would be changing my life forever.

I got to the room, and I sat down to get my blood pressure taken. I was wearing a "Ripndip" beanie to cover my cold, bald head and a purple sweatshirt from Ripndip also that had a lot of cats on it. The room was cold. The nurse began to take my blood pressure and heart rate, and they were super high. I was nervous and anxious but had a good reason to be.

The doctor walked into the room and introduced himself to my mom and me. He sat down with us, but he did not seem friendly. He was an older man with thin brown hair and a socially awkward demeanor. He was a genius, but he came across as rude. He started to explain the long-term and short-term effects of radiation. As he listed the possible complications, both present and future, my heart pounded faster and faster. He said I would have a higher risk of heart disease, skin cancer, and almost every other health issue imaginable. It would have been faster if he had told me what I would not get from radiation. I was scheduled for four days of radiation. The immediate side effects were awful: mouth sores, nausea, hair loss, fatigue, vomiting, and more. I listened to Dr. Hall's half-hour speech about how everything could go wrong. I fought back tears and wanted to scream. How would I survive this? He gave me a paper and made me sign a consent form for treatment at Baptist Hospital under his supervision. I felt like I had signed away my soul to the devil. Dr. Hall left the room, leaving me in turmoil. I broke down in tears, panic, and fear. "How will I ever live a normal life again?" I screamed. "Will I even live?" I cried hysterically, and my mom hugged me. The nurse in the room also said some encouraging words. But I was terrified. I would have to get my heart, teeth, lungs, blood, skin, and every other organ checked every six months for the rest of my life. I had not understood this before. I did not know that cancer, chemotherapy, and radiation would cause long-term health issues and damage my body permanently. I thought that chemotherapy and radiation would only harm me temporarily and that once I was done with treatment and cancer-free, life would go back to normal. But I faced the reality of my situation that day. I had to overcome this mental barrier that was causing me so much anxiety if I wanted to live.

After I had finished the consultation for radiation treatment, it was time to begin the simulation. My mom and I left the room and were taken to a place in the hospital called "Proton therapy." The hallway was long and cold. There were several rooms to the right of the hallway that were patient rooms, and to the left of the hallway, there were about six gigantic rooms, each of them with a huge opening and a thick metal door that looked like an elevator door, and in these gigantic rooms were machines that looked like spaceships. These were the rooms where radiation and proton therapy occurred. The room where they did radiation was almost as big as my house. There was a thing that looked like a metal detector in the front of the room, and right in front of it was a humongous machine that looked as big as a spaceship, with lasers that were pointed directly at this metal detector-looking object. The metal detector-looking object was the thing I was going to be standing under and holding onto during my radiation treatments, I soon realized, and the gigantic space-ship machine that had scary-looking lasers pointing at me was how I was going to be receiving radiation. I was shocked. I could feel my heart drop. I was going to have to be alone, in this room, standing up for 30 minutes while radiation went through my body. I could barely grasp this concept.

After I had gotten a good enough look around and begun to process this, a few doctors/nurses pulled me over to the side and told me it was time to begin measuring my body. I was confused. Why would they need to measure my body? These doctors had all the tools. They had markers, rulers, and tape measures. They began to mark my body with dots and draw on my skin with markers, taking measurements of my lungs, height, waist, and just about any measurement you could possibly take on the human body. These doctors and nurses were not talking to me. They were just measuring my body and reading the measurements out loud so that they could take note of my body and prepare lung blocks for the radiation treatment. It felt like a science project. And I was the one being tested on. I felt inhuman; I was still in shock at the side effects and long-term effects of radiation, and now I was processing everything that I had just seen in the last hour. Finally, after 30 minutes of standing still and having my body measured, they were finished. These nurses and doctors were taking my measurements so that they could make lung blocks and block my lungs from the radiation while I was receiving it. This was disgusting. I felt violated; I was covered in marker and was just told that radiation was going to mess me up for life.

However, my day of torture was not over yet. Doctor Hall wanted me to do an MRI. This was my first time doing an MRI in my life. I was taken into another conveniently gigantic room in the hospital and placed down on a bed alone in a room and put under a gigantic white donut-looking machine. I sat there for about 10 minutes, feeling the claustrophobia that this machine gave me and having anxiety that made me feel like I was going to scream for help at any second, but finally, it was over. The machine stopped making whirring noises and started to quiet down. The door of the room was opened, and I was finally done. Was it time to go home yet?! Yes, it was. But before my Mom and I went home, we were introduced to someone very special.

Her name was Barbie. She was the child life specialist at Baptist. Because I was being treated mainly at Nicklaus Children's Hospital, I was given a child life specialist to help me cope with the treatment that I would be receiving at Baptist. Barbie was an angel. She made this day not so horrible after all. She talked to my mom and me for a while, and we had so many questions that she answered about radiation. I was really nervous about having to stand for so long. How was I going to stand for 30 minutes straight without taking a break? I have just finished three intense rounds of chemo. I was not exactly in good shape right now! Barbie calmed me down and told me and my mom that little kids do it almost every day. And so did older people. "Everyone that comes here for treatment gets their treatment," she said. "No matter what, even if you are weak and tired, they will figure it out." I felt a little bit relieved, but I was still super anxious about this. Barbie gave us her number and told us to text her if we had any questions.

We finally left the hospital and took the 45-minute car ride home.

When I got home, I was so anxious. My anxiety was through the roof. Nothing could get the words "radiation" out of my mind.

I hated it. I was scared, I was frightened, and this was making me so anxious. I tried everything to get my mind off of radiation, but it felt like nothing worked. It kept me up at night, made me cry, made me mad, and made me sad. I was scared because I knew that the only way for me to live was to face this challenge and stand up in a room all alone, receiving the most toxic treatment to your body in the world: radiation. It wasn't like any other challenge I had faced in my life. I could not just tell myself, "Okay, I don't have to do it if I really do not want to." I had to do radiation; it was my only hope of survival.

The days went by, filled with blood transfusions, platelet infusions, and countless tests at Nicklaus Children's Hospital. I had to prepare for the bone marrow transplant, and that meant doing all kinds of tests: CT scans, pulmonary function tests, EKGs, chest scans, abdominal scans, and another bone marrow biopsy to check if I was still in remission. One morning, I had to drink four medicated Powerades in less than an hour and then have a CT scan. It was horrible. I was in the patient room when the nurse came in. It was around 7 a.m. on Monday, October 5th. She said she could not use my port for this scan. She would have to give me an IV. I had not had many IVs since I got my port, but I was not afraid. I lay down on the bed, and the nurse wrapped a blue band around my arm. She tightened it as much as she could, squeezing my bicep. I winced in pain as she tightened it more, trying to find a vein in my arms, which were flattened by chemo. She said, "Oh, I think I see one!" She kept the band on and grabbed a needle from

CHEMOTHERAPY

her supplies. She inserted it into one of my veins. It hurt more than I remembered. But she did not stop, even when the vein seemed to collapse. She kept poking around in my vein with the needle. I cringed in pain, trying to be strong. But I couldn't. It hurt too much. "Stop," I said slowly, and she looked at me and took the IV out. Blood dripped from my vein, and she pressed a bandage on it. She said she had to try again. She moved to my other arm. She wrapped the band around my other bicep and aimed for the same vein as before, but on my right arm. It was the same as before. She missed the vein, and I was in pain again. I was so frustrated. Why couldn't they get a vein? The nurse left the room and came back with another nurse. The new nurse insisted on trying on a vein in my hand. It worked. They did it. It was painful, uncomfortable, and gross, but they found a good vein in my hand. They placed the IV, and I was off to do my scan with contrast. The scan was fine. It was just normal to me at this point. I was used to all the tests, scans, biopsies, and things that came with being a cancer patient. I just didn't like pain or uncomfortable situations, which is pretty much everything cancer treatment is.

After my scan, I had to get my teeth checked at a dentist. It was routine to get this done before a transplant. I went to the dentist, and all my teeth looked fine. I had a few teeth that were pre-cavities, and the dentist just padded them with some filling, and I was fine. But the real thing that worried me after the visit was my wisdom teeth. They were slowly coming in. I was so worried. Am I going to have to get them removed before my transplant?!

Would this delay my transplant and possibly let the cancer come back!? I was freaking out on the car ride home, and I was still super anxious about radiation. I felt stuck. I felt my mind was working against me. I just wished I could stop thinking so much for a while. I understood too much, and it was bad for me.

My next great adventure came on October 16th. My transplant was delayed a week because my blood counts still needed to recover. But on that day, I had to go to Baptist Hospital to test out the lung blocks that were made for me. It was time for my first real simulation of radiation. It was not the real thing yet, but it felt just as scary and real. The room was prepared as if it was go-time. There was a speaker, and I was told I could connect my phone to it through Bluetooth and listen to music while receiving radiation. This is pretty good, I thought. This is really going to help me stay strong through these treatments. After all, music was free therapy to me. It was time to prepare the lung blocks and test them out. Several nurses surrounded me. They began to place the lung blocks in front of me. The lung blocks were literally the exact size of my lungs, and they protected them from radiation. But these lung blocks were placed on a glass cover in front of me, not on my skin. That meant I could not move during treatment. Because if I moved, the lung blocks would be ineffective, and my lungs would be hit with radiation. This could damage me or even possibly kill me. I really didn't know. But I knew it was real shit. Real shit that I was going through. It was life or death, and I knew when the time would come for radiation, I would have to stand as still as possible and be able to get through it. But today was just a simulation. No real radiation was going to be hitting my body.

After what felt like hours of standing still under a giant metal detector-looking object and having the lung blocks placed directly in front of me, it was time to start the simulation. Everyone slowly walked out of the gigantic room. The door shut closed, but it was not a door. It was more of a sealed door, like something you see in movies. It was like an elevator door, only sideways and sealed extra shut to ensure no one would receive this toxic radiation besides me. I was alone in the room, the door was shut, and I was scared. I was not allowed to move. The front side of the lung blocks was tested, and it went well. After a few minutes of being alone in the room, the doors slid open, and it was time to switch sides. I had to turn around to test the backside of the lung blocks. They turned me around, and this time, I was facing a wall, not the giant spaceship-looking machine, and viewing the gigantic room. I was about 6 feet away from a wall, and behind me, the radiation was pointed directly at me, and the lung blocks were placed on my back this time, not in front of me. Everyone left the room again, but I felt more tired this time. I kept telling myself to push through, but I couldn't. I fell down, and everything became blurry. The doors rushed and opened the door. Before I hit the ground, the radiation coordinator, Linda, grabbed me. And then everything went black.

I remember opening my eyes to see about 40 people in the room. All nurses, doctors, specialists, and people that I did not know. I was so confused. What had just happened?! I was on a stretcher in the room, and nurses were huddling over me. I was hooked up to air through my nose. My finger had something on it that seemed to be either taking my temperature or my blood. I was so confused that I could not tell the difference. I was still in pure shock from what had just happened. I was drenched in sweat. The nurses took my glucose levels and asked me if I was okay. I told them I was okay. I was super scared. The nurses wheeled me to a different room called the PACU. PACU stands for Post Anesthesia Care Unit. I was alone in this unit, and my mom eventually came to the room. She sat next to me, her eyes teary and full of fear. I could tell she was just so happy to see that I was okay, though. The nurse took my glucose level and then asked me if I had eaten anything. All I had that morning was some pancakes. But it was the afternoon, and I did not have time to eat lunch before the simulation. That is most likely why I passed out. So I decided to get some food. I ordered a sandwich and had a nice drink with it. After that, I was discharged from the hospital and able to go home.

Once my mom and I got in the car, I began to cry. I was so scared. I thought to myself, how was I going to do radiation if I just passed out during a simulation? I was freaked out. But at the same time, I felt more comfortable in a way. I had gotten pretty close to the radiation team at Baptist, and the nice lady named Linda seemed to really care about me. It was like my worst-case scenario with radiation just happened. Everything I had feared had just come true, but for some reason, it felt good. I felt less anxious. I felt like the people doing my radiation treatments now know my fears and how fragile I am so that when I actually have to do the real thing, I will be okay.

My mom and I stopped at Starbucks on the way home. I wanted to get a caramel frappuccino, and I really think I deserved it. It was a tough day. I was tired and wanted something that was good and would make me happy. The frappuccino was really good. When I got home, I was so tired. I sat down on my bed with my cat, Oreo, who was dying slowly of diabetes, and I cuddled with her. Oreo was my comfort animal. She licked my bald head as we both were in my bed, watching the rain come down on this Florida afternoon in October. Oreo got sick with diabetes just about the same time that I got sick with cancer. It was like she felt that something was wrong with me. She hated seeing me sick. Oreo was not just my cat. She was like a mother figure to me in a certain way. Whenever I would cry, break down, or be sad, she would notice and come cuddle with me. Oreo was a family member to me.

CHAPTER FOUR

THE BMT

On Monday, October 19th, I was scheduled to be admitted to the hospital for a bone marrow transplant. This was the day I had been waiting for and dreading for a long time. The day that would change my life forever.

The day before, I celebrated my brother's 21st birthday with him. His birthday was the day before my long-awaited bone marrow transplant admission to the hospital, otherwise known as my last days of freedom, before I faced the grave unknowns of a bone marrow transplant. Who knows what could happen in that unit and if I would come back as the same person? We spent the day together and got my brother's favorite cheat meal—McDonald's. It was the final supper, the last time I would eat McDonalds and be able to tolerate it. But I did not know this at the time. All I knew was that I enjoyed the fries, the ketchup, and the chicken sandwich.

The next morning finally came. It was time to leave home for a while. I packed my bags with my mom. It felt like we were going on a vacation, but we weren't. We packed suitcases full of clothes, snacks that I could tolerate, posters, and decorations for my hospital room, which would become my home for the next month and a half. It was all real. It was actually time. I had been so anxious about the radiation and the transplant, and it was all going to start today. Today, I was going to be admitted to the hospital, and the next day, radiation would begin. I would have to undergo radiation twice a day, every day, from Tuesday to Friday—four days of it. Then I would have a "day off" and then begin super intense chemotherapy to completely wipe out any remaining cancer and destroy my old bone marrow so that there would be room for a new bone marrow, room for the transplant. So that there would be room for a stranger's blood from Germany to become my new immune system.

Today was also an emotional day. Oreo was also being put down. Her diabetes was becoming too much to handle, and she was miserable. We had to do it. A lot was happening today. It was the last time I would ever see Oreo in my life, and the last time I would ever step foot in this house and have one set of DNA. The next time I come home, I will be a different person with new DNA, new lessons learned, new complications, and a new life ahead of me that I was not prepared for. But I was unaware of all this. I was just scared of radiation and hoping to get it out the way, get my transplant, become cured, and go back to surfing and the gym.

My mom and I took our final goodbyes, looking around the house and seeing everything we would miss for a while. I hugged and said goodbye to my sister, Jennifer, my brother, and his girlfriend, Maddy, who was living with us at the time. We walked outside the doors to our Blue Honda CRV and got in. Steven, Jennifer, and Maddy were all outside, waving goodbye to us. We rolled the windows down and said our final goodbyes. It was time to face the next chapter in my life. I immediately thought of my dad, who passed away from cancer over four years ago. He would be so proud of me. My father needed a bone marrow transplant, but he passed away before he could get his. I was doing this for him, surviving for him. I love you, Dad. This is for you, I thought, and we drove off to the hospital.

We arrived at the hospital, and it was time to be admitted. We got to our room in the 6th tower, but this time, we were in the bone marrow transplant unit. It was sealed off from the other units in the hospital. It was only VIP guests allowed, I mean only transplant patients with no immunity allowed. It was on the 6th floor, along with the other oncology patients, but the rooms for BMT were separated and sealed off, and not many people were allowed in and out. The rules for BMT were pretty strict. You couldn't leave the unit. It was about six rooms, two nurses' stations, and a small kitchen for parents. The room I was in was freezing cold. It was a large room, though, and waiting for me in the room was a Lego set and a cat blanket, courtesy of the amazing child life specialist "Ellie." It was nice that there was a Lego architecture set for me to build and a blanket. I felt a little more at home.

It was time to get my port accessed, get labs drawn, and begin this journey.

I needed a blood transfusion because my hemoglobin was low. After the transfusion, I ordered my final meal from a restaurant. It was my last chance to enjoy food from outside the hospital since I would have to avoid bacteria and protect my low immunity. I chose pizza and savored every bite. Then I went to bed and just sat there, staring at the ceiling. Tomorrow, everything will become real. I would start radiation and begin my journey with the transplant. I felt a mix of fear and hope. I knew this was the final step of treatment, and soon, this would all be in my past.

I was woken up multiple times during the night because the nurses had to take my vital signs every 2 hours. I barely slept. It was an awful first night in our new home. But at around 5 am, it was time to get up, get dressed, and go to radiation. I walked to the bathroom, dragging an IV pole attached to my port, and put on some socks, a shirt, and a sweatshirt. I tried to shake off the drowsiness. The ambulance was here. I left the room, detached from my pole, and two men in EMT uniforms and gear laid me down on a stretcher. They took me to the elevator, downstairs, and into the ambulance. It was my first time being in an ambulance. I felt somewhat special. It was kind of cool, despite the early hour.

Radiation treatments started as early as 7 a.m., so we had to get to Baptist Hospital quickly. I made sure to eat a snack this time so I wouldn't pass out like I did in the simulation.

We finally arrived at Baptist at around 6 a.m., and I was wheeled down from the ambulance in the stretcher and taken to the front door. From there, my nurse, my mom, and I walked to the radiation center called Proton Therapy. It was all familiar to me: the long hallways filled with patient rooms to the right and the radiation treatment rooms to the left. My mom and I were placed in a small, cold patient room. We asked the nurses for blankets, and I came prepared with a sweatshirt. It was even colder than Nicklaus Children's Hospital, and let me tell you, that place was cold. This hospital was a glacier. We were freezing. After about 20 minutes of waiting in the room, there was a knock on the door. It was Jackson. Jackson was a bald, super nice African American dude. He was another one of the people doing my radiation treatment. He and Barbie (the child life specialist at the Baptist hospital) were there and told me it was time for me to start treatment. I had to leave my mom in the room alone and face radiation all by myself with a whole bunch of strangers that I somehow had to trust my life with. I was ready, though. I brought my own speaker and was going to connect to my phone via Bluetooth so that I could play music while receiving this disgusting treatment. I already knew all the side effects, and I knew that the treatment would build up in my system, so the more I did it, the weaker I would get. This was my first treatment, and I had to be strong and get through it with ease so that I knew the other treatments would go well.

It was time. I had to be shirtless for radiation. I took off my shirt and began to walk into the room. Nurses followed and brought markers, a glass shield, lung blocks, and an X-ray that would take pictures of my lung blocks to make sure they were in place before they could start the radiation. I stood there, surrounded by nurses, shirtless, bald, and sweating, even though it was freezing cold. I stood under the big metal detector-looking object, put my hands down by my side, and gripped the sides of the objects around me. There was a bike seat under me, just in case I had to sit down or was going to fall. There were cameras in the room, and I would be watched while receiving the treatment, and they would talk to me to see if I was fine. The code was "Blink once if you're fine, Blink twice if you are not."

They began to take pictures using the X-ray to figure out where exactly to place the lung blocks. Once they got the right picture and it was in place, I would be ready to start, but first, they had to draw on me with a marker and mark where they put the lung blocks for the next session. After nearly 30 minutes of standing still, holding on to the pole's sides, it was time to start. My music was playing, and the door was shut. I was all alone, and all I could hear was the whirring of the gigantic laser projecting onto me. My Spotify playlist, called "BMT," was playing in the background. I listened to "Back in Black" by ACDC, "Californication" by Red Hot Chili Pepper, and other songs I found motivational and meaningful. I just kept holding on and waiting for each song on my playlist to finish so that I could get closer to finishing my first treatment. One song went by, and another one went, then another one, and finally, I heard the radiation team say the words, "You're halfway there, you're doing great, blink once if you are OK." I blinked once, and then all I could hear was, " I walk a lonely road……" It was "Green Day" playing. It hit me in the heart. I was alone in a freezing cold room, standing, sweating from my armpits, bald, shirtless, and hoping for life. The song gave me motivation but also made me feel my emotions. I was really doing it. I was really receiving radiation, and it felt horrible. I was receiving the most toxic treatment known to mankind, and I had to accept it if I wanted to live. I thought about Oreo and the fact that she was going to be put down. I knew she was dying to give me all of her strength so that I could push through this rough treatment.

But my thoughts were soon disrupted, and I heard, " Only a few minutes left, and you're done. Blink once if you are okay." I blinked once. I kept listening to the music for motivation, feeling every lyric as if I was running a marathon and needed the motivation to keep going. But instead of a marathon, I was receiving radiation, holding onto a pole, and standing up for my life. All my favorite motivational and emotional songs were playing. I felt every lyric in my heart as I held on to the pole and kept standing.

After 15 minutes, that seemed more like hours, I heard. "You can sit. We are finished," and the gigantic elevator doors that separated the nurses from possible radiation exposure and I opened. The lung blocks were taken down, and I was put on a bed. I was so happy to have finished the first treatment. I was wheeled back to my room and reunited with my mom. Boy, was I happy, and I had a lot to tell her. My mom had been amazing. During this whole journey, she had been right by my side through everything. She was happy to see me, and I was so glad to be with her.

I got back to the room, and it was freezing cold. I was excited to have finished my dose of radiation. But I was far from finished, and I knew things were going to get even more difficult as the radiation accumulated in my body. I was just happy to be back in the room, though. My mom and I talked and even put on the T.V. in our small room. My mom sat on a chair 2 feet away from my small bed. She was covered in blankets. *Pawn Stars* was playing on the TV. We ordered some lunch from the hospital menu and waited for it to arrive. The nurse soon arrived in my room and brought me my mid-day medications. All these medications were new to me. It was part of the pre-bone marrow transplant regimen. I had to wait a few hours to receive my next radiation treatment. I finished with the first session at around 8:30 a.m. and had to wait until midafternoon for the next treatment. This gave me time to relax in the room, recover, eat, and mentally prepare. But honestly, it was a little boring, and it made the day drag on. I watched *Pawn Stars* and *Storage Wars* all day. It kept my mind off things. It was nice.

But after a few hours of relaxation and some food that made my stomach feel gross, it was time for the next session, the last session of the day. After that, my first treatment would be complete. Jackson knocked at my door with Linda. They asked if I was ready to go. I said yes, and they offered to take me down the hall on a stretcher, but I said I would walk instead. They insisted on me going on the stretcher, but I felt fine walking, so I walked to the room. It was time to take off my shirt, connect my phone to the speaker, and prepare to stand still for another 30-40 minutes. It wasn't the radiation treatment that was the long part; it was the setup for the treatment. Every time I had a session, the doctors had to take pictures of my lungs using an X-ray to make sure the radiation was not hitting my lungs. This took about 20-30 minutes every time. And the worst part, I could not move. You had to be still, or else you would have to restart and place the lung blocks in the right place over again. This was for my sake, though. If I moved, my lungs would be hit by radiation. I had to be still. My life depended on it.

Finally, after multiple markings on my lungs with markers, many X-ray pictures, and nurses trying their best to have small talk with me, it was time for the second session of the day. It was the same thing as the first session. I stood tall, waiting for each song on my "BMT" playlist to finish so that I could keep track of time. I thought, okay, "Way Down We Go" By Kaleo just finished playing. That's about three and a half minutes gone by, a few more songs, and we are halfway there. Each radiation session was about 15 minutes long. I just had to get through around 4-6 songs, then I would be finished. I kept waiting to hear the words "You're almost done" or "Blink once if you are okay," but this time, I did not hear it for a few minutes. I started to worry, but then I took a few deep breaths.

Then, to my relief, I heard the words, "You're halfway there. You're doing great!" I felt relieved. I had so much anxiety about this situation. I had fears that made no sense. It sounds ridiculous, but I was scared of being in this room alone and the door possibly malfunctioning or something going wrong. Being alone gave me so much anxiety, and I hated it. But it taught me that I was stronger than I ever thought. I was doing it. I was doing radiation. I was standing still, focusing on my music and not passing out. Yup, that's an important one for me.

Finally, after about 15 minutes, the gigantic doors began to open, and the radiation machine that looked like a big white spaceship stopped making whirring noises. I was done for the day. Thank God. Day 1 of radiation is in the books. I was escorted back to my room and reunited with my mom. It was time to go back to Nicklaus Children's Hospital. But we had to wait for transport to come first. This would take some time. My mom and I waited in the freezing cold room. After about an hour of waiting, more *Storage Wars*, and some laughs between us, transport finally arrived. We were reunited with our nurse and some EMTs, who escorted me out to the ambulance on a stretcher. I was placed in the back of the ambulance and taken back to Nicklaus. It felt amazing to arrive back at the 6th tower of Nicklaus. It was home for me, way more comfortable than Baptist. Baptist was an adult hospital; the people were super nice, but it was different. I knew everyone at Nicklaus, and I truly felt loved there.

It was time to go to sleep. I needed to rest. We ordered some disgusting hospital food off of the TV menu with the small remote attached to the bed, and I showered. I had clear instructions when I showered, though. I was not supposed to get the marking washed off my body. They had to stay so that during the next few days of radiation, the team would know where to put the lung blocks. Before I got into the shower, I had to get a blood transfusion. I walked into the bathroom, attached to my pole, which was full of different medications being vigorously pumped into my body. The line hanging down from my port, connecting my port and my body to the pole, was bright red and full of blood. My body was being pumped with blood from a bag attached to my IV pole. I looked like a damn science experiment. I was bald, a bit bloated, with pale skin, a port in my chest, markers all over my chest, covering my lungs, showing exactly their size and location on my body. The marker on me was a solid red, with underlying blue marks and a plus sign in between each of my lungs. It was all so real at that moment. I was not the same tan, blonde, athletic surfer I used to be. I felt like a bald science experiment. My identity was lost. The shower was so uncomfortable. Trying to wash your body and not getting your port or pole wet felt like an Olympic sport. I was tired. But finally, I was done showering. In the hospital, showers are not something you typically enjoy. You do them to stay clean from infection. They are never comfortable or satisfying, and I realized that I would be showering, attached to an IV pole every day for the next 4-6 weeks or however long I would have to stay before I could go home.

 I was tired, and after the shower, I sat in bed and ordered some hospital food. Hospital food was horrendous, but it was all I was allowed to eat now because of the rules of BMT. I am not allowed food from outside the hospital because of either food poisoning or bacteria. It was a difficult thing, knowing that your diet was going to suck and that radiation builds up your system. But I was motivated, and I kept my positive attitude. I was ready to sleep, and I was also ready for tomorrow.

I had to get up at around 5:30 a.m. after a long night of barely sleeping. Nurses were doing the usual vitals every 2 hours and blood work at around 5 a.m. It was the schedule. The no-sleep BMT regimen, huh? Not so much fun. The room was freezing. It was October 21, 2020. I had to gather every ounce of strength to get out of my bed. I was tired, it was cold, and I was comfortably wrapped up in my blanket. I gathered the strength to get up, go to the bathroom, throw on some clothes, pee, and face the day. It was going to be another challenging, long day full of ambulance rides, freezing rooms, bad food, and radiation.

I was picked up again and taken in an ambulance to Baptist Hospital. As I looked out the back window of the ambulance, I could only see cars behind us and the roads we already passed. It was weird to only see out the back window and not be facing forward in a car. I was placed on the stretcher in the back of the ambulance, tied down by some light straps to keep my body from moving or falling at every turn. I wore the same thing as yesterday: a purple Ripndip sweatshirt, purple Ripndip socks, and some shorts. We arrived at the hospital at 6:30 a.m. My mom and I got to our same room as yesterday, and I quickly ate a Blueberry

Nutrigrain bar before my treatment to give me some energy. I wasn't that hungry, but I knew I needed to eat. Soon enough, it was 7 a.m. Jackson and Linda knocked on the door while I was talking to Barbie, and it was time to start again. Day 2, treatment 3 and 4 of TBI (Total Body Irradiation) is what the treatment I was receiving was called.

I was brought into the room, and it was time to repeat the same thing as yesterday. I got under the large metal detector-looking object and grabbed onto the side poles, and scooched my butt right above the bicycle seat in the middle of it all. It was a really awkward setup. My port was still accessed, just not attached to a pole. I was shirtless with markings all over my chest and was as bald as Mr. Clean. Not a single hair on my head. It was time to take photos of my lung blocks and make sure they were in place. Before that happened, I put my phone down on a shelf a few feet away from me, connected it to my Bluetooth speaker, and began to play my iconic playlist, "BMT," on Spotify. I was listening to the most motivational, hype, sad, and emotional songs I knew. It was a whirlwind of emotions, but it brought out the strength in me in every session. Just hearing Green Day, ACDC, Machine Gun Kelly, Imagine Dragons, Jack Johnson, and all of my other favorite artists motivated me and made it feel like radiation was a workout.

After 20 minutes of photos and finally getting the lung blocks in the right place, all the radiation therapists and technicians left the room, and the giant machine pointed at me began its menacing course of treatment. I could not look down during treatment or move my head. I had to stay still. However, this time around, I felt a little shaky and tired. But I held on tight and did my best to stay still. After a few minutes, I heard, "Blink once if you are okay." I blinked.

Then, a few minutes later, I heard the most anticipated words, "You are almost done. You got this." Then, finally, after 15 minutes, the machine stopped whirring and making weird noises, and I was finished with the front of my body. I was taken back to my room, and Jackson was so proud of how well I did. My mom and I waited a few hours, ordered some not-so-great lunch, and watched the tiny TV in our freezing cold single-bedroom patient room. Finally, It was time for my next session. This session would be the back of my body receiving the radiation, and I would be facing the other way, this time not looking at the machine but facing a wall instead. It made the room look small because all I could see in front of me was a wall, and all I could hear was my music playing. This session hit me harder. After I finished this second session, I felt way more drained, less energetic, crappy, and tired. But I was finished with two days of radiation, and it was time to go back to Nicklaus Children's Hospital and rest. Transport came and picked my mom, our nurse, and me up, and we were headed back to camp after another long, cold day at Baptist. When I got back, I was weighed, and it seemed I had gained some weight. I was retaining fluids. It is the protocol to get weighed two times a day and have your vital signs checked every few hours when you are in the transplant unit.

The doctor in control of my medications and treatment was Dr. Godder. She was an older, experienced, veteran BMT doctor. She had tons of experience and was one of the pioneers of Bone Marrow Transplants with 50% matches. Luckily, I had a 100% match. She was a tall, older Israeli lady who had served in the army. She was tough but also loving. I was her last transplant patient before she was going to retire. She was really nice to me for some reason. But she was strict. She stuck by the book and the old way. When she saw my weight after I came back from Baptist, she ordered a medication called Lasix. This was a medication that made you pee—I mean, it really made you pee.

I got Lasix through my pole, and in the next few minutes, I was peeing clearly and peeing a lot. I was tired and did not feel like getting up from my bed to use the bathroom every 30 seconds. I had a few urinals at my bedside and filled them up quickly. Lasix sucked. I hated it every time I got it, and it was going to be a part of my future as well. Dr. Godder ordered Lasix twice a day for me! Are you kidding me?! I was so annoyed, but I had no choice. I had to accept it and keep pushing forward. I had no time to ponder how annoying or unfair things felt to me. I wanted to surf again; I wanted to be okay and alive, so I had to deal with the pain and suffering now.

That night, I started to feel the side effects of radiation. I was really tired, but I still had to manage to pull myself out of my bed, walk to the bathroom with my pole, receive another blood transfusion, take medications, do my daily mouth rinses, and try to eat some food. My appetite was a little lacking, but I still managed to eat some dinner. I went to bed that night exhausted. I was woken up about four times during the night for vital signs and temperature checks. It was so annoying. Every time I would get comfortable, I would hear the door slide open and have a blood pressure cuff wrapped around my arm, and I would wake up.

It was 6 a.m. again and time to go to Baptist. This was day 3. I only had two more days, but today was going to be harder. On top of the TBI I was receiving the last two days, I would be receiving two additional lung blasts of radiation each day, meaning today I would have a total of 4 sessions of radiation. After the radiation, then I would just stay at Nicklaus and receive the rest of my treatment and my transplant there. I just had to get through the next two days of radiation.

It was another classic 6 a.m. ambulance ride, the usual. I wore the same thing as always, prepared for the freezing cold, and ate a bar in the ambulance to get some energy before my treatment. We arrived at Baptist at around 6:30 am as usual. My mom and I got to our freezing cold room, and we were greeted by Barbie, my child life specialist. She is amazing. She told me how well I was doing and that because tomorrow was my final day of radiation, she had a surprise for me. I was excited about it and wondered what it would be. While all the radiation therapists were setting up my lung blocks and adjusting the handles of the bar I held on to, she talked to me. She kept me awake and alert, which was a big help, considering it was 7 a.m., I had barely slept and was tired.

She was a very special part of this process, and I appreciated her so much. She left the room after a few minutes because she had another patient to attend to, but the nurses and radiation team had gotten to know me at this point, and they were really nice to me.

My phone was hooked up to my speaker via Bluetooth, and the morning session was about to consist of front-body TBI and my first session of Lung blasts. It went well. As usual, I played my music and pushed through. But I was exhausted. The lung blasts consisted of me lying down on a bed with a giant machine over me, giving radiation to my lungs. The afternoon session was the same. First, I received TBI on my backside, and then I laid down on a table and received the lung blasts, all while listening to inspirational music that pushed me through the intense fatigue, nausea, low blood counts, mouth sores, and vomiting that radiation-induced on me.

We got back to the hospital that night, and it was just more of the same: more medications, more infusions, more blood work, more vitals, more Lasix, more peeing, more exhaustion, and less appetite. Tomorrow was my final day of radiation, but I felt no excitement, only a longing for it to end. I was woken up at 5:30 a.m. again and taken to Baptist by ambulance as I had done many times before, but today, I was given a sweet surprise. The wonderful and sweet child life specialist, Barbie, dressed up as a huge inflatable cat to surprise me. She knew I loved cats, so she thought it would be funny, and it was. It made me smile, and I got a huge kick out of it. The treatments went smoothly that day, just as they always did. It was tough, but I kept my head up and stayed my course. I completed my final fourth radiation session that day and, in total, had done 12 sessions.

Radiation was hard. It taught me a lot. I learned that sometimes in life, we think we can't do something, like stand still for 30 minutes without moving while weak from chemotherapy and anemic. But we can. I was nervous and so anxious, but for some reason, I was strong when I needed to be. I was able to get through all 12 sessions of radiation. It made me feel horrible, but it's not a peculiar feeling. We all have something in life that we must do, but it terrifies us, and we try to avoid it. Sometimes we succeed. Sometimes, we choose the easy path and remain in our comfort zone, but our comfort zone never leads us to greatness. I was forced out of my comfort zone and had to deal with my major fear of being alone, my major fear of radiation, and my major fear of being too weak to get my treatment. But I did it. Radiation was harsh, painful, disgusting, and unbearable. However, I persevered and completed all my radiation treatments. I had so much anxiety about radiation, and it haunted me constantly, but after I completed all my radiation treatments, it was out of my head. I felt accomplished like I had finished a long paper for school. But instead of school, this was life or death. The radiation team even gave me a small medal and a Lego set because they were so proud of me. It was a great gift, and it meant so much to me. This treatment I had feared since the day I was diagnosed and told I would have to receive it. I felt like I had won, but I did not know the struggles that were next for me. I was unaware of how hard my next chapter would be in this journey.

Chemotherapy: ATG (Atgam) and Bone Marrow Transplant.

The next step was chemotherapy and the bone marrow transplant. I was going to be receiving chemotherapy called ATG, or Atgam. It was the highest dose they could possibly give. The whole idea was that they wanted to wipe out my old bone marrow completely, get me free of any remaining cancer cells, and eradicate my bone marrow to leave room for the new cells to be infused into me, to give room for my stem cell transplant. I thought this chemotherapy was going to be a breeze.

I had a "day off" after I finished radiation, in which I did not get any chemo; I just got infusions of fluids and medications. But this is when the radiation side effects really kicked in. I started to be super exhausted, and when I received the chemotherapy days before my transplant, I would have to get my bedsheets changed every few hours because I was sweating through them. At night, I remember sweating so much and having such bad fevers. When I started the chemotherapy, I was given another line. I was given a PICC line, which is a long catheter that is inserted into your vein that carries blood to your heart. It was placed in my arm, and it was done so that I would have two lines, the PICC line, and my port. I had to have two lines in case something went wrong with one of them during a possible emergency. Yeah, transplant is serious. No messing around. Everything was sterile and clean. It had to be. I was going to have no immune system for a few weeks until my new marrow kicked in. That was the scary part. Any possible infection, bacteria, sickness, or anything could be fatal. I was not even allowed to leave my room until I had enough white blood cells.

The chemotherapy infusions went fine, but I had heard that it was not the first days of chemo that were hard; it was the days after. After I received this crazy, intense chemotherapy, I was ready for my transplant.

The day was October 27th of 2020. Today was going to be my new birthday, a day when I received a stranger's stem cells—a stranger from another country who signed up to the registry and decided to save a life. The day began somewhat early in the morning. My doctor, Doctor Godder, was in the room. I was given a ton of IV Benadryl at the time the stem cells were infused into me, so honestly, it did not feel like a big deal. I was too groggy, and I was halfway sleeping through the whole thing. The day was a blur, and I was exhausted from 12 draining sessions of radiation and days of the most intense, menacing chemotherapy known to man. I barely remember anything, just the doctors and nurses coming in and giving me a paper that said, "Happy Transplant Day." But the next few days were when it all really hit me. It became real. And I realized this was not going to be easy. The chemo I received was nothing like the chemo I had gotten before during my cycles of chemo. The Atgam, mixed with radiation, was a total monster. It tortured me. I had mouth sores so bad that I had to be put on an IV drip of morphine 24/7 for the pain. At first, I rejected the idea of a morphine drip. I wanted to be strong, and I did not believe that the pain was going to be that bad. I mean, I had been through chemo the last few months anyway. How different could this be? It was different.

The side effects of the chemotherapy hit me so hard. I had mouth sores that were so painful that every time I swallowed saliva, I would need a push of morphine. I was unable to eat, so I was hooked up to TPN, total parenteral nutrition. I had a whole tree of IV poles; they all just stacked onto each other, and every time I got up to use the bathroom, I had to drag these heavy poles with me. I was having severe hallucinations as well. Every time I closed my eyes, I would see myself in the room, and it would be like someone was there with me besides my mom and the nurses. At one point, I even asked my mom, "Why is Mack here?" Mack is my grandma's boyfriend. He was also most definitely not in the room with us. The side effects were horrendous, and the next few weeks were honestly a big blur to me. I was constantly receiving Benadryl and morphine for various reasons, so I was sleeping and vomiting nearly every other hour of the day. It was treacherous. I even popped a blood vessel in my eye from vomiting so much. I was unable to use my phone, computer, or watch TV because of my eye and also because of how nauseous I was.

My biggest struggles of the day consisted of getting up to shower or going number 2. It was awful because I had sores everywhere. Yes, everywhere, and that includes my anus. The bathroom was painful. I would be in excruciating pain every time I went. There were days when the nurses offered to clean me in my bed instead of me getting up to shower, but I refused to be this way. I managed to gain strength and get up every day to shower. I would drag my tree of IV poles with me to the bathroom, throw an aqua guard on my port and a diaper on my PICC line, and attempt to shower. There was a day that I went to shower, extremely exhausted, beaten, and drained. I got up to shower and went to the bathroom. I looked in the mirror at my pale, skinny, bald self and said to myself, "You are going through this for a reason. You are strong. You can do this". I sat down on the chair in the shower and told myself, "I can't do this," then I stood up, gathered every ounce of strength left in me, and took the damn shower. It was just a shower. It meant more to me, though; it was a testament to my true strength, and I had to reach deep down to gather all of that strength. After I took the shower, I felt so accomplished. Like I just ran a marathon or lifted a new Personal Record in the gym. I was so proud that I could still get up and shower on my worst day.

My next challenge after these crazy side effects was engraftment syndrome. Because I had a transplant from a donor, my body seemed to reject the transplant a little bit. This was not good. I was hallucinating so much that I found myself talking to people who were not in the room. I would be playing a game on my phone, and then I would open my eyes and realize I was just holding my hand up and my phone was not actually there. I would be eating and then open my eyes and realize there was nothing in my hand. I was not actually eating; it was all a hallucination. It was scary because I was half asleep and knew in a way that I was hallucinating, but there was nothing I could do about it. I had so much swelling in my heart and lungs from the engraftment syndrome that the doctors feared for my life at this point, but a miracle happened. I made it through the syndrome somehow.

The doctors started me on IV steroids, and it solved the engraftment syndrome, but it left me with excruciating pain in my back, making me need more pain medications. The biggest thing for me at this time in my transplant was waiting to engraft. I was given these cells from a donor, and little by little, these cells have to make their way into my marrow and engraft. For days, my white blood cells would be 0,0,0, and then little by little, you would see 0.1 white blood cells. Every day, it would come up a little bit, and every day, I would get further to fully engrafting and having enough white blood cells to be able to leave my room and walk the halls. On day ten post-transplant, I began to engraft at 0.1 WBC (White blood cells). The next day, 0.2 WBC. Finally, my mouth sores began to get better. The white blood cells were slowly creeping up, helping repair my mouth and giving me a tiny taste of an immune system. Those weeks in the transplant unit were all a blur until the last two weeks. I was on so many pain medications, dealing with so many different pains, sores, and complications that I was very forgetful. But the last two weeks of my five-and-a-half-week admission for my bone marrow transplant were more memorable.

The bone marrow transplant unit rules were strict, but as I was starting to engraft and was able to get out of bed more, I felt more alert, and the hallucinations were gone. For those whole five and a half weeks I spent in the bone marrow transplant unit, every time I went to the bathroom, I had to pee in a urinal and poop in a hat. Everything that came in and out of me was measured. It was disgusting, but it became second nature and a part of my life, just like the tree of poles attached to me by the port in my chest and the PICC line in my arm. Every sip of water and every ounce of food I put into my mouth was recorded and sent to my doctor. Everything was so strict and intense, and it had to be; it was just the rules of transplant. I had to tell the nurses literally everything. It was hard to do, but I adapted to the situation, and it became my normal. My mom and I even had a chart on the whiteboard in our room as to how many liters I had peed during the day so we could tell the nurses, and they could chart it.

As I was engrafting and getting some white blood cells, the sores started to go away, and I started to be way more awake and cognitive during the day. I was still exhausted and spent most of the time in bed, but every day, my mom and I would go for a walk. We were finally allowed outside of the room, and even though I had to wear a full gown, gloves, and a mask, I was allowed to walk the floors of the 6th tower again. I was able to leave the Bone Marrow Transplant Unit and walk past the glass doors that separated me from the rest of the oncology patients. Walking was a lot harder than I remembered it to be. I would walk one lap around the floor and have to come right back to my bed to rest. But I pushed myself every day because I wanted to be stronger and get back to being on my feet. Being in bed all day, knocked out on pain medications, was not a life for me. I loved the outdoors and being active and social, which was why this was such a challenge for me. I had to let go of my identity as I knew it before. I had no choice. This was my life now. I was a transplant patient and was very aware of how fragile my body was. I am not the healthy, muscular, tan blonde, tall, athletic surfer I once was. I was a cancer patient, learning lessons in life that some people never learn.

My brother would come to visit me every day. My mom, my brother, and the nurses were all I had in the hospital. I had friends who texted me and kept in touch with me, but human contact is just much more enjoyable and real to me. Every day when my brother would come, I would perk up and feel better. My mom even joked that whenever Steven would come by, he would fix my pain and suffering. I always felt better when he was there. We would build Legos together and make the craziest ships we could possibly make. He would bring the Lego bin from home, and together, we would bond. At 19 years old and 21 years old, my brother and I were kids again. We used to play with Legos when we were really young. But this sickness, this transplant, brought us closer than I could have ever imagined. We would walk, and my brother would encourage me, motivate me, and keep me strong along with my mother. My brother had a buzz cut because he was consistently shaving his head to be bald with me. My brother is not the best at expressing his emotions sometimes or relating to me, but he loves me so much and has always been there for me.

After four long weeks in the unit, I had not been outside once. But my doctors are amazing, and they wanted me to get some air. I had not had a breath of fresh air in a month. The child life specialist at Nicklaus Children's, named Ellie, took me outside for the first time. I had to wear a full gown and a mask, and walking to the elevator, getting in the elevator, and walking outside felt like a whole marathon. It was the furthest I had walked so far, and it was not far at all. It really showed me how weak I was. But at the moment, I did not care. I pushed through, and I was outside for the first time with this new immune system after my transplant. I was still attached to my pole, wearing my favorite Ripndip beanie. My mom told me, "Breathe, baby," and I took my Ripndip mask and my beanie off. I exposed my head to the sun and my body to the wind. It was a moment of joy, a moment of recognition of how far I had come. It was weird to be outside, but fresh air was something else to me. It was amazing. After being cooped up inside for so long and facing death, I came outside and appreciated life. I did not care that I was bald and weak. I was just grateful to be outside. After being in a sanitary, clean, and sterile room for nearly four weeks, I felt alive. It was a miracle, and it felt like one of the best moments ever. It taught me that sometimes we just have to take a breath and realize that we are alive and that we have so much to be grateful for.

After a minute or so, my adventure came to an end. I was tired from standing for a few minutes and headed back upstairs. That day was my most memorable day during the whole five and half weeks that I was admitted for my bone marrow transplant.

The room that we had in the transplant unit was our home at the time. Directly sitting from my bed and looking at the bathroom door, there was a quote on a poster that read," It is not about what happens to you. It is about how you react that matters."Every day when I was in pain, struggling, and felt bad for myself, that quote lifted me up. In the transplant unit, while I was undergoing my transplant and trying to accept this new marrow, I could not control anything that happened to me. All I could control was how I was going to react and adapt. We always had music playing almost every moment of the day. It was healing to me, and my mom and I tried to make our environment as healing as possible because we were there for a month and a half.

    I was finally able to go home after five and a half weeks in the hospital. But the day I was discharged from the hospital was not an easy day. The nurse practitioner, Maylin, came into our room and began to explain the very intense rules and the insane amount of medications that I would have to be taking at home. The rules for going home were super strict. No visitors, every meal I ate had to be cooked very well, and I had to stick to a non-bacterial diet. I was taking medications at certain times during the day, and some medications even three times a day. I was not allowed in the sun. I had to always wear a mask when outside and shower every time I got out or came back from the hospital. I had to wash my hands constantly. I was not allowed any food from restaurants or takeout. I could only eat home-cooked meals and processed foods. I could not miss a single medication. We had to have someone come and do a deep cleaning of our house before I went home. I was not allowed to go anywhere besides home and the hospital for the next

100 days. Full on quarantine. I had to come to the hospital three times a week for the next few months. And every medication I take has some not-so-fun side effects. I was so scared to go home.

I threw on my favorite Miami Heat jersey, a Bam Adebayo one, took my Ripndip pillow in one arm, and grabbed my green Ripndip backpack. My mom and I waved our final goodbye to the nurses, took the elevator downstairs, and went to the garage. My mom was dragging our suitcases full of clothes and hospital decorations. We packed them into the car and gave each other a look of excitement and fear because we were going home. Going home and getting into a car was a shock. Seeing vehicles on the road, other people, and the normal setting of life felt weird. It was overwhelming, and after being stuck in a hospital and only going outside a few times, the real world was scary. It was full of dirty, unsanitary things that could possibly cause infection. It was scary to go home to an environment that was not the hospital. The hospital had become my home. It was my comfort zone, and it was safe there.

CHAPTER FIVE

THE FIRST 100 DAYS

When we first arrived home, my mom put the car in the park, and we just looked at each other, unable to move. We were so shocked, and it felt weird to look at our house and know this was our home again. We got out of the car and went into the house. My brother and sister were not home, and the first thing I saw was my cat. I was exhausted. Being in a car and walking from the car to inside my house drained me. I was super weak. So I sat down on the couch, and my mom unpacked everything. But the most amazing thing happened next: Kitty sat on my lap. I had not seen her in over a month and a half. And now that Oreo was gone, Kitty was the only cat we had left. I loved her even more and appreciated her small cuddles so much. It was so healing and therapeutic to be around Kitty, an animal. It felt amazing, and I was just so happy to be with her. She was my comfort animal. But I was nervous to have Kitty sit on my lap; I was worried about the bacteria that she could be carrying and the possibility of her getting me sick. But it was healing and worth the risk.

Just because I was finally home did not mean that things were easy. I had one job: to take my medications, drink plenty of fluids and eat. It shouldn't be too hard, right? But it was. Eating, drinking, and holding down medications was a lot easier said than done. I had tons of abdominal pain, and I was so weak. People were happy for me and assumed that I was home from my transplant, so things were all good now. But that was not the truth. I was so weak, and I wanted to recover fast. I tried to work out, but I could barely do it. Lifting 3 lbs was a mission, holding down food was a mission, and showering was a mission. I would be so weak in the shower that sometimes my mom would sit down outside of the bathroom door and wait for me to get out to make sure I was okay. I could tell she was holding back tears every time and worrying about the frail state of her son.

Every time I wanted to walk outside, which was only in the evenings because I could not get any sun, I had to wear a mask, even if there were no people around. Sleeping was so difficult as well. In the hospital, they would give me medications to help me sleep and take away my pain, but at home, I did not have that. I was in so much abdominal pain from a medication I had to take called magnesium that sleeping became a challenge. You would think that because I was so tired, I would sleep, but I was constantly nauseous and in pain. But I always tried my best and picked myself back up. I wanted to walk around the block around our house, so I tried. But I failed. I could only walk a few meters past the house. My nurse practitioner told me the first two weeks at home were going to be the hardest. She was right. I had to come into the hospital on Monday, Wednesday and Friday. But after only a few days of being home, I was readmitted to the hospital. I had so much stomach pain. I was in the infusion unit that day, and I was feeling horrible, so the doctors admitted me. It turns out I had GVHD. Graft Versus Host Disease. Basically, my graft, which is the new stem cells in my body, was attacking me, the host. GVHD targets major organs. It targeted my skin this time, and I had GVHD of the skin. It presented itself in a rash on my skin, thighs, and arms. I had identical rashes on each arm and each thigh. Dr. Galvez placed me on oral steroids at a higher dose and gave me cortisone cream for the rash. It was my first complication after my transplant. It felt normal, though. I had just kind of assumed that everyone got this. Thankfully, after a few days in the hospital, I was discharged and able to go home. I felt a little bit better. I was able to eat more and walk more. This time, when I was home, I pushed myself and finished the walk around the block. It felt like a marathon, and my breathing was heavy at the end of it. But I did it, and I felt proud. I was getting stronger, finally. I was doing a small workout every day and shooting some hoops in my backyard. We lowered the hoop to 8 feet, and I shot from 3 feet away, but it was still progress. I was still bald and skinny at about 140lbs. But I began to channel my strength and motivate myself to get stronger, using all my setbacks as motivation. Little did I know I had a huge bump in the road coming my way, another major setback.

I noticed that every time I would eat, I would have to go do number 2. Everything that was going into me was coming right out almost immediately. I was losing liters of poop a day. It's gross, but it was true. On Christmas day, I had to be readmitted to the hospital. I spent my Christmas evening in the hospital, but thankfully, I spent Christmas morning at home with my family. I also spent Christmas Eve at home. I felt like shit. But I appreciated eating a Christmas Eve dinner with my family more than I ever have in the past. I was so happy to be at home spending time with my family that I kind of forgot about all my health issues, and I felt happy again. I appreciated my family, the love, and the wonderful scent of being home. We had a super nice dinner together, had our Christmas traditions, and shared our love for each other, but I knew I was going to have to go back to the hospital.

It was my second time getting admitted to the hospital through the ER. When my Mom and I got there, I was placed in a small room, and the residents came in and asked me about my symptoms, but before I could finish the conversation, I had to use the bathroom again. I was taken up to the 6th tower. My hairline was coming back because it had been over a month since I last had chemotherapy. I was happy to be done with chemotherapy. My hairline was prominent, and so were my eyebrows coming in. That made me feel more human when I looked in the mirror. But I did not know how serious my situation at hand truly was.

I got into the room and had to poop in a hat. I had pooped liters that day, which could be fatal. It could lead to death. The doctor at the hospital that night, Dr. Maher, immediately started me on TPN (Total Parenteral Nutrition). He took away all my eating and drinking rights. Everything had to be through an IV. For the next two weeks, I had to stay in the hospital, not eat anything, and be placed on the highest possible dose of steroids: 60,60. 60 mg in the morning and 60 mg at night. Yeah. It sucked.

The next morning, I had to have a colonoscopy and an endoscopy done. I was in the minor procedures suit for this procedure. It was thankfully quick, and I got back upstairs by the late afternoon. It was another mental hurdle as well as a physical one. I had just gotten home a few weeks ago, and now I was back in the hospital. I began to worry.

My GI GVHD was really bad. It was life-threatening. But it was weird because I did not feel bad at all. The doctors ordered me to be on total bowel rest. No food at all. Just IV nutrition. The worst part was IV nutrition did not fill you up. I was on steroids at a super high dose. This meant I was hungry all the time. Steroids give you a huge appetite. It was painful because, for over a week in the hospital, I could not eat. But finally, my doctors allowed me to eat some food. I was put on a super strict diet: the GVHD diet. I was only allowed to eat rice, saltine crackers, and plain chicken at first. But let me tell you, those saltines were freaking amazing! Then, I was allowed to eat sugar-free Jell-O and sugar-free Powerade. Plain white bread was my dessert. It was amazing. They tasted like heaven. It was the best thing I had tasted in months. Talk about appreciating stuff so much more when you don't have it. It felt like heaven to eat those saltines. I appreciated it so much because, at one point, I had nothing. I was not allowed to eat at all. That's my point here: With everything I have gone through, cancer, chemotherapy, the transplant, nearly dying two times already, I saw life in a different light. I was spoiled before all of this. I was a healthy athletic surfer who could eat anything my heart desired. But I did not appreciate it all. But when I got taken down to this low point, to GVHD of the GI, to being stuck in a hospital bed for over a week on nutrition through an IV. A new perspective came upon me. It was like a third eye had opened. And for some reason, I did not care that I was bald, sick, and had complications. I was just happy to be able to eat some damn food. I was also beginning to feel a little stronger, and every day, my brother would come visit me. He would bring 3lb weights for me, and I would do some bicep curls, some shoulder presses, and other exercises with the light weights. I was doing it attached to huge IV poles, but my brother and mom motivated me to do it. It helped me get out of bed and made me feel better. We would work out in our heat jerseys. I would wear my Bam Adebayo jersey, and Steven would wear his Kelly Olynyk jersey. I am a huge Miami Heat fan, if you can't already tell. I love basketball, and it kept me entertained while in the hospital, along with the wonderful nurses, doctors, and, of course, my family.

My mom and I were finally able to go home after two weeks in the hospital, but I had to go home on the GVHD diet. The truth was, I was so hungry that it was not even bad. I liked eating plain food. I just began to appreciate every moment and piece of food I had so much more because of where I had been previously. It was the first time in so long that I was eating a good, healthy, balanced diet. During my transplant, I was unable to tolerate any food at all. But my abdominal pain, nausea, and vomiting had disappeared with this strict diet and high dose of steroids.

The steroids saved my life once again. But steroids were a deal with the devil. They made me have terrible insomnia. I would sleep about 2-4 hours a night, then I would be ramped up with energy all day but be tired at the same time. There is no way to really explain it. Those who have been on a high dose of steroids know the feeling. It's awful. I was always hungry. At this point, my hair had started to come back, but I looked nothing like myself. I was bloated, with a buzzcut, and my face was huge. This was all thanks to the steroids called Prednisone—the worst. I hated them. I felt better, but I was so self-conscious. I looked horrible. I had a gigantic moon face and was half bald. I lost all my confidence, but at the same time, I felt amazing. I was getting stronger and lifting more weight every day. I was playing basketball in my backyard (with a mask, by myself, still not much immunity). I was using the stationary bike almost every day. But I felt like an alien when I looked in the mirror. It was hard, and I was in a conflict with myself. I really appreciated feeling better and stronger, but I looked awful and was not sleeping. It was just weird. I was still going to the hospital three times a week, but I would come home every night. I would never be tired, even if I did not sleep. It was awful. I just wanted some sleep. I tried everything: sleep meditations, medications for sleep, mindfulness, no technology, and deep breaths. But nothing worked. The steroids were just too strong. The steroids also gave me leg pain and stretched my skin so quickly that I began to have scars in a lot of different places around my body.

One hundred days after your transplant is a huge milestone. This usually is the time when the doctors take you off the immunosuppressants or lower the dose so that you can start to build some immunity. But for me, my day 100 was not a celebration or a huge milestone. It was just another day. The doctors did not even put it into consideration lowering my medications. I had GVHD twice, and it was bad. So, I needed to stay in a bubble and quarantine for a lot longer than most people after a transplant. I was frustrated but humbled. I had to let go of dates. I had to just appreciate that I was alive after everything I had already gone through. GVHD of the GI, HepatoSplenic Lymphoma, transplant, radiation, chemo, engraftment syndrome. Not a lot of people would still be alive after all of that. I was lucky. I was grateful and put things into perspective. I knew that my normal would come back one day, but it was going to be a long time from what was expected. I had to force myself to be patient, humble, and appreciative of the amazing support system I had. But I was able to find light within all the struggles. I realized I needed to share this with people. My story was inspiring, and helping inspire others started to become my hobby.

However, at this time, I had a lot of body image issues. I overcame my body image issues by learning other ways to feel good about myself. There was simply nothing I could do to change my body or my circumstances, and I know how difficult it can be for you as well if there is something you don't like about yourself and you cannot change. We, as humans, all have these issues. I began to stop taking a bunch of photos of myself. I also stopped using social media and comparing myself to others who had not been through what I had been through. I learned that no one is the same. Some people are just born different, and it's not your fault. During this difficult time, I had friends ask me if I was eating a lot of candy, but as you know, I was eating a bland, very healthy diet. It was simply medications and my circumstances making my body look this way. So, I took these struggles and stopped thinking about what I looked like. I started to do things to feel good. I learned that looks do not matter; what matters is how you feel. I adapted to my situation, and I suggest you do the same, too.

In the beginning, when I was getting my hair back, my body was gaining weight, and I was looking extremely bloated and had a moon face, which made me sad. But if you are going through something similar that makes you feel like your identity has changed and that you do not look like you once did, I suggest you avoid making the same mistakes I did. Just realize that you do not have to go through cancer, a bone marrow transplant, and GVHD to learn that you are not the same as everyone else. I wish I had learned this earlier. I wish that cancer did not have to teach me the life lessons it did. But I am grateful it did teach me and humble me. So that is why I am writing this book. I want to show you, through my personal struggles, identity crises, and pain, that life can still be enjoyable and that you can learn to appreciate the things you have around you. Practices like physical activity, walking, talking to a friend, and being vulnerable and open can help you. I have come to understand that physical activity, such as weight lifting, even light weights, and small workouts, have greatly improved my mental health. I suggest you do the same if you are going through cancer or something tough, just finding the strength to get out of bed and be in control of something in your life while everything else seems to be in God's hands and the doctor's hands.

CHAPTER SIX

THE AFTERWARDS

The first 100 days after my transplant were not that great, but I was still alive. Times were not changing, though. I was still going to the hospital, the infusion unit particularly, three times a week. Then, all of a sudden, one of my blood counts began to drop. My platelets were super low. My doctors diagnosed me with TMA (Thrombotic microangiopathies). This was the destruction of red blood cells, low platelets, and possible organ damage. On top of that new diagnosis, my liver enzymes were starting to get higher. This is why I was going to the hospital three times a week. Medications that are in the form of pills are hard on the liver, but if they can be infused as an infusion instead of a pill, it might not stress the liver as much. This was my doctor's opinion, at least.

But it made things tough. Going to the hospital three times a week does not sound like much, but I was there all day, receiving a medication called Micafungin and getting my labs drawn every single time.

I was frustrated. It was day 100 after my transplant, and I wanted to be better already. I wanted to be able to jump again, surf again, see my friends, go in the sun, and have a life. But my health made me be patient. The dose of steroids I was on made it super hard to sleep, and my knees were in pain because of the steroids. I had a friend come over and sit outside with me. The first thing he told me was that I looked bloated. It broke my heart, but I am sure he did not mean to be rude. It was just rough. Seeing someone with whom you used to do normal things was rough. It was rough to look at someone who had everything you desired and good health.

I found myself in a time where I was struggling mentally to identify who I was. I was coming out of a bone marrow transplant. I was on high doses of immunosuppression. I felt great but looked awful. I had some hair now and did not look like the cancer patient I used to look like. I felt like an alien at moments. I had to teach myself and learn that being alive was a blessing and that I have to appreciate life and everything I have. It was not easy. My identity felt lost. I could not surf, swim, go in the sun, or hang out with my friends, but I did not feel sick anymore. It was a confusing time. I was going to the hospital three times a week, getting my port accessed every time and getting the same room in the infusion unit every time my mom and I would go in.

BEYOND THE BLOOD: A STORY OF LOVE

My mom and I had this bond at this point that made us inseparable. We had been through so much together, and we were always together. It was amazing. I was so happy to have her by my side. She is the best. On days when steroids would give me horrible mood swings and insomnia, and I would feel ugly and bloated, she would still comfort me and love me. She went every day with me to the hospital, and she drove me because she loved me so much. She could not bear to see me go to my treatment alone. The nurses at the hospital loved her so much, and we bonded so well. My mom and I were best friends. She and my brother encouraged me to start sharing my story to help motivate and inspire other people. I started off by sharing some posts on Instagram, but then my brother highly encouraged me to make TikTok videos. I was not a huge fan of TikTok at first, to be honest. But I started sharing my story there, showing other people and cancer patients that I was still here and working out. People loved the strength that I showed on TikTok, and they were inspired by the videos I shared of me working out during my treatment. It made me feel like my struggles were worth something. People really appreciated me sharing my struggles and being open. It opened a whole new world for me, a world where I could inspire people by just being me.

TikTok helped me a lot, but the time in the hospital was still tough. From January 2021 to April 2021, I spent three days a week in the infusion unit of the hospital, balancing medications, dealing with TMA, and trying to figure out the issue of my liver enzymes rising over time. After a few weeks of receiving my TMA treatment, I was doing much better. My platelets and hemoglobin began to stabilize and come up again. Finally, the TMA was getting better. But there was a little girl in the hospital that we knew that was not doing as well as me. She had TMA, but it was really bad. I had some extra vials of my TMA treatment, called Soliris, also called Eculizumab, left over that I was not using at the time. My doctors called my mom and me and asked us if we would be willing to give my extra vials to this patient in need. Of course, we said yes. They could not give us the name of the patient because of hospital policy, but my mom and I already knew who it was. We had been in the transplant unit at the same time as this little girl and her family. My mom got to know this little girl's parents, and they were always texting each other and asking for updates. My mom knew it was this little girl named Fiona because she was in contact with Fiona's parents, and Fiona was not doing well. Fiona was in the PICU. She was in critical condition and needed a miracle to survive. She needed this medication that I was taking, and we gave it to her. We had no updates for days about Fiona, but we knew she was still alive, and we continued to pray and think of her.

When we came into the Hospital the next week, my Mom texted Fiona's mom, and we met up and talked to her. My mom gave her a care package, and we heard wonderful news. Fiona was doing better. Fiona's mom was so grateful that she gave me and my mom a huge hug. It felt so good to know that a patient who was in a similar situation to me at one point but got super sick was still alive, and they had hopes for the future because Fiona was doing better.

BEYOND THE BLOOD: A STORY OF LOVE

My TMA was under control, and my GI GVHD and skin GVHD had all pretty much gone away. But for some reason, my liver enzymes kept rising. My doctor, Doctor Galvez, and my nurse practitioner, Maylin, were always concerned. On March 18th, 2021, I had a really concerning talk with the nurse practitioner of the bone marrow transplant clinic, Maylin. She was concerned I had liver GVHD or an infection in my liver. If this turned out to be GVHD of the liver, I would be on immunosuppressants for even longer. I felt very sad and anxious about my future. I was scared about my liver and wanted to know If I would be okay and what the next step was in my treatment plan. I felt like I had run out of ideas for TikTok and videos, and I was also a bit stressed about school, but I knew that my health was way more important. I just wanted to see my friends and be normal again, not be bloated or worried about the sun, and be able to do fun stuff again. Still, I knew I was going through this for a reason, and this fight was not for nothing. It is just so difficult living life day to day with no real plans for the future and never really knowing when my body will look good again and when I will look like myself again. There was just still so much uncertainty that it gave me a feeling of anxiety and stress. I was trying to be as positive as I could, but some days, it is hard, and I feel like I just want to run into the ocean or run somewhere far away and get away from all this medical stuff and doctors. I love them; they saved my life, and I am beyond grateful for that, but some days are so hard. Some days are just so frustrating. I want to be done by now and return to the things I love. I have already struggled enough, and now I have to deal with this whole new liver GVHD thing.

I had to be admitted to the hospital for a liver biopsy. I had to have an MRI the day before the biopsy to check on my liver and make sure the surgeons knew where to go in during the procedure. The MRI was very interesting. They had to poke me 3 three times to find a vein for the contrast that they would use during the MRI. I had so much anxiety while doing the MRI, but I stayed calm and tried not to have a panic attack and freak out even though I was close to losing it in the beginning because of how claustrophobic it felt there. I had to wear headphones, and there was a loud banging sound every time they took photos during the MRI. They also made me hold my breath for certain amounts of time, 18 seconds, 12 seconds, and other periods of time I have forgotten. I was there for about an hour. It was wild. It felt way longer. I hated MRIs. I am super claustrophobic. Inside, the machine felt so small, and I was closed in, so I shut my eyes half the time and prayed that no one would forget about me, and eventually, the MRI would be over, and I would be free. When I got back upstairs to my hospital room, I was so happy to be done with the MRI. I felt so free.

However, spending the night in the hospital again was awful. I barely slept and felt super crusty all night. I had to be NPO the next day, meaning no food or drinks after 12 a.m. until I was finished with my procedure. I hoped the procedure would be early in the morning so that I could finish it and then be able to eat or drink because I knew I was going to be really thirsty. I waited all morning, hungry, tired, and moody. Finally, at 12 pm, the transport came and picked me up, and it was time for my procedure. I was so exhausted but happy to be going downstairs for my procedure finally. I was taken into the minor OR. I looked around, and everything was so familiar. I was used to this scene because of the countless bone marrow biopsies the surgeons had performed on me in the minor OR. The surgeons and nurses were beginning to pump me full of anesthesia. But I had a good sense of humor and loved to always say something funny before I was knocked out. I said, "Good luck, guys." I don't know why, but for some reason, I always get a kick out of saying some final words before I go under for a while. It was fun because none of my procedures had ever gone wrong before, and I wanted to let the surgeons and nurses know that I really appreciated them.

I woke up super groggy, as usual, in the recovery room in the minor procedures suite and was taken upstairs back to my room. I had so much pain in my throat, stomach, and head, and I was nauseous. I was not allowed to leave the bed for 8 hours. There was some weird reason for this because, after this procedure, you had to be in bed. The nurse wrapped some weird thing around both my legs that would squeeze them tight and keep blood flowing into my legs so my blood did not clot. It was really weird, but it also felt good. I was not allowed to get up, so I couldn't shower. I felt super crusty and disgusting. I had been operated on, and my port was accessed. I was just uncomfortable, and it was gross. But thankfully, the next day, I was able to go home. I was not allowed to work out for a week, which really sucked.

THE AFTERWARDS

I went home the next day, and I was so happy to be home. After spending three days in the hospital, I appreciated home again so much. It was insane. I was not attached to a pole, I could shower without my port being accessed, and I was free! I was still waiting for the results of the liver biopsy to see what was causing my liver enzymes to rise, but I was not worried about that. I was focused more on being home. I was so happy to be home, eat my mom's home-cooked meals, and not have to eat the horrible hospital food. Unfortunately, I was not home for long.

On April 4th, I woke up in the middle of the night feeling sick. I had to go to the bathroom. I began to throw up. I was throwing up so much, and then it turned to diarrhea. It was awful. I felt so sick. I kept vomiting and pooping, and it was non-stop. My mom called the hospital. She was talking to the resident on call, and they told me to come to the ER. The whole car ride to the hospital, I was vomiting. I threw up in the car on the floor. It was gross. I felt horrible, and I had so much stomach pain that I was screaming. After a long 30-minute drive, my mom and I arrived at the ER. I was so weak that I could barely walk. I dragged myself from the car to the Emergency room entrance, holding onto my mom for dear life with a bucket in my other hand. My mom checked me in, and we sat down on the comfortable chairs in the waiting area. I vomited into the bucket in front of everyone in the ER, and people were staring. But I did not care. I was in so much stomach pain. I had to go to the bathroom. I think I actually shat myself. I got to the bathroom and exploded with diarrhea. It was gross.

After getting out of the bathroom and back to the waiting area, they called my name. I was rushed to an examination room in the ER, and I was a priority because I was an oncology/bone marrow transplant patient. It was 3 a.m. at this point, and I was in 10/10 pain in my stomach/abdominal area. It was horrific. It was one of the worst pains I had felt during my whole cancer journey so far. It was not as scary as radiation, but it was way more painful than any mouth sore I had before.

The nurse in the ER accessed my port and gave me some morphine for the pain. It really relieved me and made me feel better. An hour later, after waiting in the ER examination room, I was taken to an ultrasound room. I had an Ultrasound and an X-ray done at 5 a.m. It was not fun. I was still so uncomfortable and tired. I just wanted to sleep. At 6:30 a.m., we finally got upstairs to a room. It was already morning, and I was so tired. I did not care how bad I felt even more. I was over it. I did not care about my liver not doing well. I did not give a shit about anything at the moment. I just wanted to sleep. I was over it. I knocked out but was soon awakened at 11 a.m. I was constipated, tired, and moody. No doctor had come by yet with the results, which frustrated me so much. The doctors finally came to the room. They told me that I most likely have liver GVHD. I had to start a new medication called "Jakafi," but the good news was this was supposed to be a miracle drug for GVHD. And most people live somewhat normal lives on this drug. I was a bit excited, but I knew this drug also had side effects. It would lower my counts, which sucked. My hemoglobin was already 10, and this meant it would be lowered even more. I just wanted to go back to a normal life, have normal counts, and be around my friends. I was so mad. I was still on steroids and looked pretty bloated and alien-like still. But I was supposed to be off the steroids completely by the end of May, which really excited me. I was happy about that. This meant I would start to look like myself again! I was so happy. I had come to terms with looking bloated on steroids, but if there was a chance to get any sense of normalcy back, I was here for it.

At the end of the day, we were sent home. I spent the next few days relaxing, not working out because of the liver biopsy, and thinking about starting a class online in the summer. But the night of April 9th, I had a scary dream.

In my dream, I was back in college. But I was there with my current version of myself. I was bloated, had no immunity, and saw all of my old friends. I was around everyone, and I did not have a mask. It was a nightmare. I was having a panic attack, and I texted my mom to come pick me up immediately. My chubby face was exposed to everyone I had previously known from college, everyone who once saw me as a blonde, handsome surfer. I was sure I was going to get Covid because I did not have a mask and I was around so many people. But finally, I woke up and realized it was all just a scary dream. I realized I was scared of how I looked and wondered how I would look after treatment. Would people judge me? Was I never going to recover? Would I be on steroids for a longer time? Would I ever be able to go back into a crowd of people again? I had no answers because no one could tell me. The doctors themselves were even confused about my liver GVHD and why it was happening. It took them so long to diagnose it. I was worried and frustrated. I was genuinely scared. It seemed like no one knew what would happen to me. I was 19 years old, so young, but I began to feel much older.

A few days later, the same awful thing happened again. I threw up over 30 times in one night. I had to be rushed to the ER again by my mom. She saved my life once again. What was wrong with my stomach? I had no idea, and it really sucked. This was becoming a thing for me—being admitted to the hospital because I could not stop throwing up. I needed to get hydrated, and getting fluids through my port was the only choice.

The next morning, I found out I had to stay on steroids even longer. I was so frustrated. I just wanted life to go back to normal. I just wanted to be off the steroids and look good again, have muscles, and be handsome. I WANT TO SURF. But I did not realize how lucky I was at the moment.

CHAPTER SEVEN

LIVER GVHD, ANOTHER ROADBLOCK

How am I supposed to live like this for another six months to a year? I know, I know. I should be more grateful just to be alive, but some days, even on my best days, it is hard. I have so many little annoying side effects, and I just want to work out and play basketball again. I want to feel strong. As I am writing this, my hands are going numb. I have no idea what the side effects of everything I have gone through will be like in the future. I miss my friends, in terms of going out with them, but for some reason, I am so happy to be going through this because I genuinely believe this is the greatest struggle of my life and that I will get through this and be very happy and content with my life because I do not feel very happy today, I feel a bit discouraged and a bit down. I just want to know that I will surf again, that I will be strong enough again one day. I also want to have a nice night's sleep tonight. I am so frustrated and now I have to start a new treatment for liver GVHD called ExtraCorporeal Photopheresis (ECP).

I was just starting to look like myself again. It was the end of June 2021. I was finally off the horrible medication called Prednisone (steroids). I was working out consistently at home. Of course, I was still not allowed around people or in a gym, but I finally looked like myself again. My face had started to thin out, and my hair had grown back because it had been over eight months since my last chemotherapy. But I was still not content; my stomach was horrible, and I could barely eat any of the foods I used to tolerate. It sucked that my diet was super plain.

On July 14th, one year after my initial cancer diagnosis, I went to the hospital to meet with my doctors about the plan for my liver, and I got diagnosed with Chronic GVHD. That day, I went into the hospital wearing jeans, a nice shirt, my favorite shoes, Air Force ones, and a silver chain. I remember so clearly getting my bloodwork done and having my doctor, Doctor Galvez, come and sit down next to me in the examination room and explain to me that I had chronic GVHD of the liver. He and his nurse practitioner, Maylin, told me I had to start a very high dose of steroids again through an infusion. I was heartbroken. I had just started to look like myself again. I was just getting my confidence back, and now I knew I was going to get chubby cheeks again and be bloated after working so hard to lose all the steroid weight. It sucked, I hated steroids so much, but they kept coming back into my life and messing it up. I had to start these steroid infusions a few times a week and take a small dose of steroids at home. After a few weeks of trying the steroids plan for my liver GVHD, there was no real improvement, so my doctors recommended that I see a GVHD specialist at an Adult hospital. I was scared shitless to go to an Adult hospital after the awful experience my father had.

They wanted me to go back to Baptist, where I did radiation, and do this treatment for my liver called Extracorporeal photopheresis. But Baptist did not take my insurance, Medicaid, so I had to go to another hospital. I had to go to the University of Miami's comprehensive cancer center, Sylvester. There I was to meet with a Graft Versus Host Disease specialist named Dr. Wang. I was really nervous to go to an adult hospital. I knew it would not be the same as Nicklaus Children's. At Nicklaus, my Mom and I were friends with everyone there, and they were basically family. Everyone was so nice. We knew the nurses and doctors personally, but now I had to face a new challenge—an adult hospital. I was scared; my father was treated at an adult hospital, and I knew it was not nearly as warm as the experience that I was having at Nicklaus.

The other thing that shocked me was that before my father passed away, my family tried to get my dad to be treated at the hospital I was going to, Sylvester. Sylvester is a great cancer institute, but my father was too sick when he went and tried to get treated here, and he passed away because it was too late. The doctors couldn't do anything at that point. So, coming here was a bit sad, but it also reminded me of how similar, yet different, my dad's journey was to mine. He needed a bone marrow transplant at the end of his life to survive but was too sick to get it, and he passed away. He also tried to go to Sylvester, but he was too sick at that point. And here I was, alive. I had already gotten a bone marrow transplant, and I was going to be treated at Sylvester. It was like there was a legacy I was carrying to avenge my father and beat this disease for him. I always felt like a part of him lived on in me because I was the one out of all three kids who felt my father's anxiety and was diagnosed with cancer just like him. It's weird to explain, but I knew he lived on within me.

I met with Dr. Wang. He was a skinny, tall Asian dude. He was really nice. He was very upfront and said my GVHD was not good. We needed to start ECP soon, which was a cutting-edge treatment. The whole idea of it was to hook me up to a machine, have the machine take out a certain amount of blood, then have the machine separate the buffy coat from the rest of my blood, put the buffy coat under an ultraviolet light, which weakens it and then return the blood back to my body. In other words, this treatment was taking the cells that were attacking my liver, causing GVHD, weakening them, and giving them back to me. The whole idea was to calm the GVHD down and calm those cells that were attacking me down so that, eventually, they would stop attacking me and become normal. This treatment was to be done about two times a week for several months, and then I would be re-evaluated. The good thing about ECP was that it was not a medication. It was natural; it was just filtering of blood. But the issue is that it takes a few months to work and makes you super tired. Also, it takes about 4 hours for every treatment, so you have to be in bed and can't leave the bed for 4 hours. It was going to be tough, and honestly, I didn't really understand how it worked at first, but boy, was I soon going to understand, maybe a little too much.

In order for me to do this treatment at UM, I needed a different central line. My single port was not enough. I had to get another surgery done to take out my old port and insert a new port, a double port that was made specifically for ECP. I had to be admitted to Nicklaus again. I was going to stay a few days, get this new port placed, and have a liver biopsy done again. But this time, I started to look very different. The color of my body and eyes had changed. I was jaundiced and yellow. My liver was not doing so well. I really began to notice this the first night after my surgery for the port insertion when I peed in a urinal. The urine was straight-up brown—dark brown. Not even yellow. Just brown. My bilirubin was very high. Bilirubin is the pigment that is made during the breakdown of red blood cells, and it goes through your liver; so if your liver is not doing well and your bilirubin is high, this pigment is not broken down properly so it does not turn as clear as it should be, that is why my urine was so dark. My liver was struggling to break down and process everything because of the Graft Versus host disease attacking my liver and bile ducts. This was not good. My doctors were in a rush for me to get this port placed in and start ECP as soon as possible. It was urgent. My liver GVHD was bad.

The surgery and liver biopsy went well. But after the surgery for my port, I was so uncomfortable and in so much pain. I had to spend a few days in the hospital recovering. When I finally went home, I was still so uncomfortable. For some reason, my left leg was in so much pain, and so was my right elbow. I could barely sleep because I was still on a high dose of steroids. I was so pissed off. I had just gotten home from the hospital, and my new port was still hurting from the operation, my leg was in pain, my elbow was in pain, I could barely sleep, and worst of all, I was not allowed to work out because of the liver biopsy I had done and because of the new port placement. I was so mad and frustrated. Why is my life so hard? Most people, after transplants are done, don't get this horrible GVHD like I had. So why? I just want to be back to normal. I just want to go home, to the ocean, to the gym, to school, and to a social life. I have been socially isolated from everyone for over a year, and it was taking its toll. I was closer with nurses and doctors than I was with my real friends. It was so sad. Of course, I still talked to my friends, and sometimes they would come over and sit outside, but no one was allowed inside my house, and no one could sleep over. I just wanted something normal. I hated steroids. I wanted to sleep. I had not slept through the night in over a year now. I was always either vomiting, sick to my stomach, or dealing with anxiety. I have spent more nights in the hospital than I have at home this last year since I was diagnosed with cancer. My life was so difficult, but for some reason, I just kept going. I knew I had a purpose. I knew all my struggles and pain were going to inspire someone and that one day, this would all just be a memory, but at the moment, this serious life filled with trauma, and now, Chronic GVHD was my present. Not my past or my future. It was what I had to deal with now. I had to suffer now so that I could have a future. It was always hard to grasp, but I knew that I was going to live. I had so much support and love surrounding me that I had to keep going.

After a few days at home, it was time to start this new treatment at UM, called ECP. We were on the same floor of the hospital where I met Dr. Wang, but this time I would be going into the Apheresis unit and getting treatment. I was a little nervous but not too nervous. I got into the unit when my name was finally called after waiting for about 30 minutes in the waiting area. The unit was small, and there were only about 4 or 5 beds. It was cold, and each bed had a gigantic machine next to it, and each bed was separated by curtains. It was freezing cold, and I could see another patient on the bed lying down, receiving treatment. This patient was much older than me. It felt weird to be in an adult hospital, but I knew I had to get used to it. The nurse named "Jesus" guided me to my bed and sat me down. My mom sat in a chair next to the bed. The bed was sizable, and it was next to a giant machine. I was assuming this was the machine I would be hooked up to for ECP. The nurse told me that I was his first patient ever. I laughed and then got serious. Wait, is he being for real?! Then Jesus looked at me, and I could tell he was joking. I already knew ECP was going to be a blast because my nurse was so funny. I loved that. It made me feel comfortable. There were two more nurses in the apheresis unit, Carmen and Sergio. Carmen was an older Hispanic lady with light hair, and Sergio was an older Hispanic man with a big stomach, tan skin, glasses, and a great sense of humor. Jesus was Filipino and had long black hair that was put in a ponytail. These three nurses all seemed to be really close because the whole time when I was lying in bed waiting to start treatment, they were cracking jokes with each other. It was not like the children's hospital at all; the jokes were way more mature, but they were funny, and I loved it. But the fun was about to end.

Jesus walked over, and on the table that goes over the bed, he placed all the tools that he would be using to access my port and hook me up to the apheresis machine to start ECP. As he was unpacking his blue, sterile bag full of needles, cleaning appliances, and tubes, I could not help but notice how big the bag with the needles was. I lifted up my shirt, took the right half of it off, and left the right nipple, stomach, and port exposed so that Jesus could begin to clean the area on my port before accessing my port and hooking me up to the machine to start treatment. He began cleaning with Cholaprep, and after 30 seconds of that, it was time to access my port. Jesus got the needles that would be inserted into my chest, connected to a line that would then connect me to the apheresis machine. I almost had a panic attack. The needles were not like the 1-inch needles I was used to at Nicklaus. These needles were as big as nails and even sharper. I looked at my mom, and she went pale. We did not exchange any words. I just sat still and prayed for my life that Jesus did not miss my port. He began to bring the single needle to my chest and had to access the left side of my port with this needle. (I was going to be accessed with two different needles because the blood needs to be taken out and returned. This is the fastest way).

"3, 2, 1," he said. Jesus emphatically shoved the needle into my chest, breaking my skin and hitting the bottom of my port. It felt horrible. It was so scary. It was like getting stuck with giant needles in your chest. I mean, literally, it was. It felt so uncomfortable, and I was cringing in pain. Now, it was time for Jesus to access the right side of my port. It was the same cringing pain. No different.

"3, 2, 1," Jesus said again as I took a deep breath and felt a needle sink into the bottom of my port. I could not move. If I moved, I would bleed and risk the chance of Jesus missing my port and actually stabbing me in the chest. I had no choice but to suck it up and deal with it. After he accessed both sides of my port, he attached these lines that were like mini tubes to the needles. Jesus then flushed both sides of my port and checked for blood return to make sure it was working. He took blood from my port to check my labs and do a chemistry test, which is to check all my liver enzymes and bilirubin. Then, after attaching me to these tubes and lines that went into the needles that were in my port, he hooked these lines up to the machine. I had two lines going over my shoulder and into the apheresis machine to my right. He started the machine up, and the two lines attached to my port began to run red. Blood was being taken right out of my body and placed into this machine. I could see my blood running through these lines, out of my chest and into a machine. It was surreal. It was both disturbing and magnificent at the same time—a work of repulsing art. The treatment took time. It takes over an hour for the machine to take a few liters of blood, and then the machine has to cook the blood under ultraviolet light and return it back to me after this treatment process. It was long, about 4 hours, but I was not bored at all. Jesus was a character. So was Sergio. They kept me and my mom entertained the whole time. There was a little TV that you could watch from the bed. It only played the HGTV channel, which is like the home remodeling channel. And I joked with Jesus that it should be called the GVHD channel because most of the patients here who received ECP had GVHD. It was a good first treatment. But after one session, I realized why the nurse had to be with you the whole time; they constantly had to flush my port and adjust the machine. I was not exactly sure what he was doing, but Jesus was always adjusting something and making sure it did not go over a certain number. When the treatment was finally done, the machine stopped and slowed down. The machine was super loud, and during the beginning of treatment, it sounded like an airplane taking off, and at the end, it sounded like an airplane landing. Once the treatment was done, it was time for Jesus to disconnect me from the Apheresis Machine. He took the lines off, and all that was left were the giant nail-looking needles in my port. He had to de-access me and take these needles out of me, one by one. He grabbed his gloves, put them on, and counted down, "3,

2, 1," then he took the left needle off. I closed my eyes, cringed, and felt a similar pain as when he accessed me. Jesus immediately put gauze over the left side of the port because it was bleeding heavily. Then he de-accessed the right side of the port, just like he did with the left side. I cringed again and felt the same pain as the needle was taken out of my port. Jesus immediately put pressure on my port using gauze and was pushing so hard that I could feel my port rubbing against my upper ribs. It was disgusting, and I felt violated. But this treatment was nothing like a regular treatment or port access. These needles made your port bleed so much after. I was not used to this. I was used to 1-inch needles that would barely bleed after they were taken out. ECP was different. It was the real deal. Real big needles. Scary stuff. As if going through cancer, radiation, and a transplant was not scary enough.

After Jesus de-accessed me, he wrapped the area of my port with gauze and tape and kept applying pressure to make sure the bleeding stopped. Once the bleeding stopped, I was able to leave and go home. But Jesus encouraged me to take my time standing up. I had just been in a bed without moving for 4 hours and had a lot of blood taken from my body. I was going to be tired. And you bet I was. I was exhausted. I stood up and was able to walk to the bathroom, but I was very fatigued. After I went to the bathroom, my mom and I said bye to Carmen, Sergio, and Jesus. Finally, we're going home. It was a long day, and I was exhausted. ECP was super scary. How would I ever get used to those giant needles?! I was so tired and hungry that I did not have the energy to worry about it anymore.

I was drained after my first session of ECP, but I realized my leg was really hurting. I just continued on and tried not to think about it, but two days later, before my next session of ECP, I got home, and the AC was broken. Being sick after an ECP treatment and feeling awful at the end of summer in Miami, you need to come home to AC. I could not do it. I would most likely spike a fever if I stayed inside the heat of my house. My mom and I got a hotel, and that night in the hotel was awful. I was so frustrated. My leg hurt so much, and I could not sleep. I had a major breakdown and said that I was so done with everything. I felt like I wanted to give up. It was too much: the steroids, the ECP, the pain, the uncomfortable port, the scary needles that go into my port. It all was catching up to me. But I could not give up. I knew I stood a fighting chance. I had to continue on, no matter the pain.

After a long night, it was time to get up and go to ECP again. It was another session that was the same as the first one, but this time, I was limping and could barely walk. My left knee was in so much pain. After my second ECP session, I left UM and went to Nicklaus Children's for an emergency MRI of my knee. We called our doctors at Nicklaus and told them how much pain I was in, so they scheduled an MRI as soon as they could. I had to stay the night at Nicklaus, and I found out I had Avascular Necrosis in my left knee.

I had Avascular Necrosis, which meant there was no more blood supply in my bone. This happened because of the steroids I was on. They destroyed my bones. It was devastating to find this out. I was so young. I would have to be on crutches and a wheelchair for the next few months while doing ECP 2 times a week and going to Nicklaus the other days of the week for magnesium infusions. I had a lot ahead of me.

I did this ECP treatment for the next few months, up until October. My liver was actually doing much better thanks to this treatment. I was happy; life was not perfect, but I was doing much better. My knee still had its pain, but after a month or so, I was able to walk again. My eyes were still a bit yellow from my ongoing liver issues, but my bilirubin had come down, and my liver was starting to heal.

But then, just when I thought I was getting into the clear, I had to be admitted to the hospital for extreme pain in my stomach. It came out of nowhere. I just felt so much pain that I was unable to eat, and I felt so sick. I hoped it would be a quick trip and that I would get home soon. I came into the hospital, and I was actually right; we left after a quick few days. That was until the next day after being sent home. I felt sick to my stomach again. I thought to myself, Really?! What is it this time? We went back to the hospital. After a couple of images of my stomach and a very long day, they found gallstones in my stomach.

Initially, the GI doctors believed that with a week of IV antibiotics and a drain in my gallbladder, I would be fine. But I had seen no improvement this week, and my gallbladder was not looking good. I needed to get back to my treatment. My liver was beginning to decline every day. This had me super worried.

Without me being able to do ExtraCorporeal Photopheresis, my liver was beginning to get worse. I was admitted to the children's hospital, and they did not have ECP there, so I was only on some immune suppressant pills. My body was missing the ECP.

It really was a simple fix: Why can't they just remove my Gallbladder? Here's why: #1. It was risky with my low immunity. #2. Once you have a drain placed in you, you cannot just have it taken out and remove the Gallbladder. You have to wait for at least five weeks. This is what the surgeons told me. But there had to be a middle ground somewhere. This now diseased gallbladder was making things worse every day, and it was definitely not helping my liver. I was put on nutrition through TPN. This was also a liver-killer. But I needed it because I could not eat due to how sick I was. My liver counts kept going up every day in the hospital. At this point, I had been admitted for almost four weeks. The doctors needed to either let me go home with my drain or take out my gallbladder. So, the surgery team met up with my main doctors, and they compromised on a deal that they would take out my gallbladder. It was a risky thing to do considering the severity of my liver GVHD; it was a super sensitive area, and any mistake in the operating room could easily be fatal for me. It seemed like everything I had gone through at this point was just a joke because complications kept coming up, and I could never make it into the clear. I was desperate. I had been in the hospital for four weeks with my Mom, taking pain medications and getting fed through an IV. It was such a painful experience.

I remember a few days before the procedure, one of the nurses asked me if I was nervous, and I said, "Yes, I am." For the first time, I was actually very scared. But I knew I would be okay because I previously had procedures in the OR that turned out just fine. I had a lot of people praying for me, and I am sure that helped because I got through the surgery and was ok. Yet I knew with my liver being so bad that the next issues were soon to come.

I spent the next two weeks in the hospital, receiving morphine for the extreme pain I was in and attempting to walk when I felt I barely had enough strength to get out of bed. It was a huge challenge, and walking was so difficult after this procedure that I literally needed morphine to manage the pain and help me walk to the other side of the room to test my strength. I felt so weak but not defeated. I still had a strong motivation to get better.

The sad part was all this time I had spent in the hospital, sick, did not allow me to do ExtraCorporeal Photopheresis. I kept thinking about this because the ECP was done at a different hospital, and I could not get it done. The issue was by this point, my liver GVHD had gotten out of control. I was finally discharged from the hospital and had high hopes of ECP restoring my liver again and bringing me to health. But once again, this was not the case, unfortunately.

CHAPTER EIGHT

THE GREAT DEPRESSION

I was put on high-dose steroids again. After I was discharged from the children's hospital, I went to meet with Dr. Wang, the GVHD specialist. I did a session of ECP, and he told me I needed steroids or I would basically die. This was heartbreaking.

They started steroids, and they admitted me to the children's hospital once again. The doctors saw only a partial response to the steroids, but they continued to give me them. I was in the worst mental state of my life from January to the end of February. Things were so difficult. I hated steroids. I was anxious; they made me depressed, and they were barely working. I felt like I could not go on any longer like this. Prednisone made me miserable. It gave me so much anxiety that I got a medical marijuana license and not even the CBD Oil that we got helped. It gave me so much anxiety that not even a full dose of Ambien would let me sleep. I had become severely depressed. The main reason I was so depressed was because of steroids themself. This medication caused me to have severe anxiety and insomnia, which is torture when you are already sick. The steroids were there to save my life, but they were the true killers.

My liver was doing so poorly that my doctors demanded a liver biopsy because they thought my cancer could have come back. For this liver biopsy, I had to be admitted to the adult hospital. As usual, my Mom was right by my side, trying to keep me positive. But even with her there, it was the worst experience of my life. During that night in the hospital, a doctor told me I was having heart failure because my blood pressure and heart rate were so high because of my anxiety. I did not sleep one minute that night in the hospital. The next morning, I had my liver biopsy. Basically, they were taking a specimen out of my liver to test it for disease. The doctors wanted to know just how bad my liver really was, and this test would show them. I had my biopsy in the late morning. My blood pressure was through the roof, and they almost refused to do the biopsy because of my blood pressure being so high. With blood pressure that high, a procedure like a biopsy becomes very dangerous. Yet they did it anyway; they needed the specimen badly. The biopsy was interesting. I was wide awake. They gave me some local anesthesia and some pain meds and went straight into my liver with a giant needle. I was scared, but my anxiety was even scarier. I prayed the pain medications would give me relief, but they barely did. After the biopsy, we were taken upstairs, and my mom and I were transferred back to the children's hospital through an ambulance. It was an interesting experience, and it felt great to be at the children's hospital. But that feeling of relief soon went away when reality kicked in again. My anxiety was through the roof, and nothing could calm me down. After a few days in the children's hospital, we got the results of the biopsy. No cancer, but my liver was basically failing. The GVHD was killing me slowly but surely. I was in an awful place mentally.

This part of the next story is very difficult for me to write about and talk about. But I am just being real and want to be open about everything I have gone through.

At this point, it was March of 2022. I had been in and out of the hospital for four months. I just had a biopsy of my liver, and I knew it was not looking good. I had not seen my friends or eaten a real meal in what felt like forever. I struggled to get an hour of sleep a night, and I was done. I even told my therapist I wanted to die. She was very concerned and put me on a 1-to-1 in the hospital to make sure I did not harm myself. After a few days in the hospital with a 1-to-1, my doctors sent me home. I told them I needed to go home for my mental health. I told them I would much rather be home than in the hospital, and they agreed. I told them that my mom and I would come back in a few days. They said, "Of course. You need to."

I had tried so hard for months to be positive, but it just felt worthless. I was slowly dying, and it was the most painful thing

I ever had to endure. The mental pain was far more intense than any physical pain I had ever felt in my life. I prayed for death at this point. I hated every moment of being alive.

When my Mom and I got home from the hospital, I tried to end my life. It started when I was trying to go to sleep, and I was in the same room as my mom. I got up from the bed and told her I had to pee. A few minutes went by, and my mom noticed I wasn't back from the bathroom, so she went to check on me. She found me on the floor of the kitchen, bleeding from my neck. The first thing I saw was the pain in her eyes. She rushed me to the hospital. She immediately called the doctors.

I went to the ER, and I had to get stitches because of the cuts on my neck. It was awful being there. I was ashamed of what I did, and I felt miserable.

I was then admitted to the Hospital on the 6th tower with my mom, and we stayed there with a 1-to-1. A 1-to-1 was basically someone being in the room with you to make sure you do not try to hurt yourself. This was awful. There was no privacy even when my family visited me. Everyone on the hospital floor knew what happened to me. The worst part was when we would play music in the room, and I would see my mom cry. I knew exactly what she was crying about. I felt like a failure, and I regretted my decision so much. I was in a horrible state mentally for the first two weeks of being admitted to the hospital. I was in shock. I was anxious, and a huge part of me was even more sad than before. I would walk around the hospital with my IV pole, and I would pray that I would trip on it, fall, and die. I hated life so much. I did not want to be here anymore.

For four weeks, I was admitted. They took me off the steroids as fast as they could, and I started to only take a medication called "Rezurock." I also started taking anti-anxiety medications, one called Seroquel and the other called Lexapro. These medications actually helped me. I was also taking Ativan to get me to sleep at night. Plus, I was seeing a therapist almost every day while I was admitted. Things actually began to improve somewhat after a week and a half in the hospital. I actually wanted to continue treatment. I actually wanted to live. I stopped thinking about falling over in the hallway with my IV pole. I knew why I had this feeling again. It was because I was off the steroids. Once the steroids were out of my system, I saw things differently. I was just as shocked as I had been before about what had happened, but I wanted to get better and help myself get out of this because before, I saw no hope; life was miserable.

I started to try and do things to improve myself. My mom helped me a lot with that. She would get nurses to rush my medication. She would take me outside every day in a wheelchair and show me the sun and the outdoors to remind me that life was still here. That I still had a purpose and that there was still beauty in this world. Even when I could not see it, my mom could. She found the good in everything. She saved my life that night. She took me out of my major depression. She is the one who spent every night by my side, sleeping next to me in a hospital bed. But there was also someone else who gave me hope.

I met this "someone else" in the hospital. He was another patient. His name was Alex. We talked every night around 7-8 p.m. by the windows on the 6th floor. We would watch the sunset together. My mom was with me, and he had his brother with him. These conversations in the evenings were one of the biggest reasons my mental health improved while in the hospital. We would talk about random things and have conversations about movies and random animals. I told Alex about surfing, and he liked listening. We both had stress balls, and we often bonded over that. So thank you, Alex. Thank you so much.

After four weeks of being admitted to the hospital, my mom and I went home. This new medication I had started called Rezurock was actually doing it. It was healing my liver. I was surprised but happy. It was finally coming to an end. I was going to live, and my liver was going to get better. I was less yellow, and my skin was almost a normal color.

I was scared to go home at first. The hospital was my comfort zone for so long. However, coming home was much better than I thought. It was difficult, but going home was what I needed to really heal myself from the trauma I had been through. The first day home was a bit of a shock, but after a good night's rest, my first day at home began. I didn't know what to do. I was free from an IV pole, my port was not accessed, and the next time I would go to the hospital would be in almost a week. I had time at home. It was what I had been fighting so hard for for almost two years, but it was not what I had expected. It wasn't easy. Adjusting to being home was hard. But it was much better than the hospital.

CHAPTER NINE

HEALING

This is my journey on improving my mental health and dealing with everything I have been through. It started as soon as I got home from the hospital, and even today, I am still working on it.

The beach. Reading. Writing. Netflix. Movies. The podcast. Youtube. TikTok. Walking. The pool. Exercise. Stretching. Adventures.

Being away from the hospital is a blessing. Knowing that my liver has finally begun to improve and that I am on the road to recovery from GVHD is amazing. But it does not mean it is easy because I am home. I am still immunosuppressed, and there are still lots of restrictions and diet limitations I live with every day.

Living with GVHD is hard. There are a lot of quality-of-life issues. Yet I am still so blessed to be here. My daily routine has been pretty good, considering everything I have been through. I am mainly home all day. I still have my mental struggles and deal with PTSD from everything I have gone through. Yet I am now healing. I have learned ways to deal with these things and how to calm myself. Talking to my mom about my feelings and flashbacks has helped me so much. Whenever I feel overwhelmed about my past, future, or even the present, I talk to my mom. I tell her how I feel, and it helps me so much. My mom is always there for me; she inspires me to work out, go to the beach, go on a walk, and do things even when I feel anxious. My mom has been my rock, my best friend, and my hero. Whenever we go to the beach, it calms me. It helps me realize that I may have a scary past but can still have a bright future. That I can learn to grow from everything I have been through.

My days at home were getting better. Let me give you an example of how amazing yesterday was. The day was June 15th, 2022, and it was a day that I had expected to be great. I woke up around 11 a.m. and had breakfast, which consisted of 4 English muffins with strawberry jam on them. After I finished eating, my mom took me to get a massage. It was a wonderful massage. I was so tired that after an hour of being in heaven, I felt so sleepy and could barely get out of the bed. After the massage, we headed home, ate lunch, and worked out a little bit.

At 5 pm, there was a special event. My brother, my mom, my sister, and I went to a place called Prestige Imports. Prestige

Imports is a super boujee car dealership. They literally say it in their name. "Prestige Imports". We know the people who run the place because of a connection we made in the hospital, and the Mom who runs it is named Valerie. She has been in contact with my mom, is a huge supporter of us, and follows our journey. So she offered for us to come to Prestige Imports and take a ride in her son's 1.5 million dollar car, called a Pagani. Her son's name is Brett, and he is one of the nicest people I have ever met. He and his family do so much for kids with cancer and rare diseases. They do an event called Ride2Revive, and they take sick kids out for the rides of their lives in supercars. That day, when we met Valerie and Brett at Prestige Imports, I went for one of the rides of my life with Brett while my brother was also having the ride of his life in a Lamborghini next to me. It was a moment like no other.

    Brett would intentionally stop his car, roll down the windows, and pull up on the road at red lights, next to Steven and Cathy (who was driving the Lamborghini Steven was in), and crack jokes. It felt like we were famous. Steven would look at me, smiling and laughing when we would stop, and people in other cars around us were taking videos of us. I guess it was pretty cool to see a Lamborghini and a Pagani racing down the streets of North Miami. So, I cannot really blame these people for being so hyped to see this. Because I sure was hyped being in that car. It was a racecar. It was so fast that when he accelerated, my head would fall back into the chair, and I would experience a feeling like I was floating or my body was lagging behind where I actually was because of how fast the car was. But one of the best parts of the experience was not the car; it was the conversations.

Hearing Brett's view on life and selling Lamborghinis was very interesting to me. I mean, this is a guy who owns a 1.5 Million dollar car. And I am someone who lives in a tiny 2-bedroom apartment on Biscayne. So, to compare the financial differences in our lives, we are in 2 different worlds. But Brett had an amazing view on selling cars. He believed and told me that he loves selling Lamborghinis to people because he is very interested in hearing people's trials and tribulations that it took for them in order to get to the point of being able to afford and drive a Lamborghini. He also told me how much he loves cars because they unite people. It was so amazing to hear how down-to-earth Brett really was. He even lost his father at the age of 19 years, and he was explaining to my family and me that he understands our struggles because we also lost our father at a young age. To see someone who is so successful, someone who is surely busy all the time working, taking this time to give my family and me an amazing experience showed me their true Character. Brett and his family were so kind to us. His Mom, Valerie, and his sister, Brooke, were having long conversations with my sister and my Mom while Steven and I were in the supercars, getting the rides of our lives. It was a wonderful experience, and Brett even offered to take me on more car rides in the future. I told him my story about what I had been through with my liver, and he seemed really touched.

It just amazed me how kind this family was, how unselfish and good they were. It really made me believe in the good in the people. I mean, this guy literally drove me in his multi-million dollar car, which he rarely drives, just so that I could have a fun time. Wow.

When my family and I got home from all of this, I was still in shock.

It was difficult to sleep that night. I felt I had come down from the amazing high that was today. I felt kind of sad for some reason. And I started to think about everything I had gone through. It took me a while to fall asleep. I was in my head, processing what felt like a lifetime of events that occurred in one day. That day, I had a massage, talked to my therapist, and rode in a Pagani. It was a day where I felt I had lived in 3 different worlds. I was in the relaxation world during the massage. During therapy, I was talking about all my trauma and explaining my mental health improvements to my therapist. After that, I was in a Lamborghini dealership, looking at some of the most expensive cars in the world. What a day it was. So much to process. Coming from basically living in the hospital to experiencing social connections and having one of my best days ever felt overwhelming and a bit unreal after everything I had been through.

But I learned that in order to rewire your brain and change your perspective on life, you must be willing to go through tough changes. I had to accept this when I first got home from the hospital. I had to accept the fact that I was getting better and that I needed to direct my mind away from the terrible things in my past and understand that even after hitting rock bottom, there was a future for me. But it all was very slow to me.

I have been back to working out every single day, but I am still at home because I am still immunosuppressed. I have taken so much away from this journey that I am still on every day of my life called survivorship. I want to encourage you and let you know that life is going to be full of challenges. It is going to be tough; sometimes, we need help, and that's okay. I could not have made it to the other side without the people around me. I was once very depressed, as you know, and I hit rock bottom. But I am saying that you do not have to go through cancer, GVHD, or all these tremendous life-changing events to help yourself grow. All these things made me grow and helped me become the person I am today. I believe that exercise, being somewhat social, and learning to forgive yourself for whatever horrible thing happened in your life will change you. I had to forgive myself for what I did. It was horrible, and it was not me. I still live with it every day, and I have learned that there is a life after traumatic events such as cancer, depression, and anxiety. There is hope. There is help. I never thought that the miracle drug called Rezurock would work. But it did. It was literally my last option before most likely passing away. Every single other treatment, I tried, but it did not work. Cancer tried to kill me, and I tried to as well. But I somehow lived. I am somehow here today. I have changed. I am not the person I used to be, but I have grown because I learned to forgive myself. I learned through tough times that you are not alone. I thought I was alone. I used to look at other people and be jealous because they were so healthy and did not seem like they had the same mental and physical struggles as me. They most likely did not, but my point is, who really knows? Cancer was something I did not wish to have to go through, but I am glad I did. Because it taught me life lessons that people do not learn until they are too old to use them. I learned that we are mortal—very mortal. Life is short. Why do we waste so much time trying to please others when we can do things that make us happy? I have been forever changed.

    I worked out during chemo. I walked during chemo. I got up from my bed every single day during my transplant. I never intended to give up when I was on the high dose of steroids, but I did. It was not my fault; it was circumstantial, and some things in life are just that way, and it sucks. But I am here, and you are reading this for a reason. There is a reason you picked up my book and wanted to hear my story. I want to let you know you are not alone. I have struggled with anxiety my whole life, and I never thought I would end up here—a cancer survivor telling my story to inspire others. But I am. It is hard being who I am sometimes. I lost my father to cancer. I got cancer, and then I went through the hardest time of my life. My dad had depression, and my dad's dad tried to kill himself. I was handed down two generations of mental health issues and given a cancer diagnosis at the young age of 19. I do not know why. No one knows why it happened, but I know it was for a reason. I want to help you become better, more motivated, and vulnerable. So many people think it is wrong to be vulnerable because you show your weakness, but it is the opposite. Being able to show your weaknesses and insecurities makes you strong, makes you who you are, and allows you to acknowledge those issues and work on them. For example, I know I have anxiety, and I know I have body image issues. Still, I work on these things with mindful practices, like eating well, less social media/screen time, being social, working out, going outside in the evening, watching the sunset, eating healthy food, and trying to get good sleep. It has been so crucial for my mental and physical healing process to get good sleep, work out, have proper nutrition, and connect with others.

Things were very smooth over the summer, but life decided that it was time for more character development. Life has been a bit interesting the past few months. It turns out my liver needed more than just one pill daily and some immunotherapy. What saved my life from the liver GVHD was Rezurock and an immunotherapy known as Soliris. I am back to ECP. They have helped me get to this point, but ECP should guarantee my liver some health. The days all feel the same. I go to ECP twice a week. I just feel so stuck, like I am still in the same phase of my life since I have been diagnosed with cancer. I still lack the immune system I once prayed for. My stomach is paralyzed. Life has decided that, for some reason, I needed to be knocked down because I needed to learn how to get back up. I have recently been diagnosed with osteonecrosis of my elbow and osteoporosis. Prednisone is to thank for my low bone density and weak joints. This medication has saved my life but made it awful at the same time. It is a fine line of appreciation that I come to call "grateful to be alive but still traumatized."

BEYOND THE BLOOD: A STORY OF LOVE

My days have been more interesting, though. I have found myself engaging a bigger audience on social media, and I have met many people. One of them is an 18-year-old girl named Najla. Najla has rhabdomyosarcoma and is not doing well. Her tumors seem to keep growing since her recent relapse. Last year, she was deemed cancer-free, but this year, her cancer has come back. Najla and I have been in contact for a few months, and we finally met up last Saturday. She reminds me of me so much. She was an athlete, a synchronized swimmer, actually, but now she cannot work out, and she is bald. She is beautiful, even when bald, and we have made some TikToks together. When I met her, she cried on her couch, and I grabbed her hand and sent her all my energy. It was a connection with someone that I had never felt in my life, knowing the fear that she has, I have felt so many times—the fear of being a young adult and knowing that you might die soon. It is not a fear I wish on anyone. It is as if you are driving a car, and someone has a gun pointed at your head. But you have to keep driving and stay calm, although that trigger can be pulled any second. It is the bullet of cancer and health issues that will eventually be released from the gun and can possibly kill us. It is only the lucky ones who survive such a gunshot known as cancer, and the ones who survive live traumatized, with great health issues and deep pain that no one should ever have to understand or go through. Being a cancer survivor is not all flowers, roses, and ringing of the bell. Yes, I am happy to be cancer-free and in remission, but the complications and quality of life that this has cost me are far greater than I have ever expected. It is a life full of social isolation, painful needles, and dozens of pills. Things do get easier, though, because at a certain point, when you go through so much, you become used to it, and doing something like being hooked up to a machine that takes out your blood, puts it under a UV light, and returns it to you becomes your normal. It shocks me to think about it, but there was once a time when I was a surfer, a windsurfer, and an athlete. There was a time in my life when I was able to eat any food I wanted without vomiting. There was a time when I could be in the sun all day, and the only negative thing would be a sunburn. There was a time when traveling was normal, and the ocean was my second home. Now, traveling to the hospital is my new normal, and my second home has become a hospital bed. Life has transitioned to something I would never see it transitioning to. But it seems that people are very proud of me and that everything I go through inspires people. My positive attitude and vulnerability have changed lives. I believe that one day, I will hopefully be back in the gym, have my joints fixed, and feel a little bit normal again. But for now, it is social isolation, hospital visits, physical therapy, and walks on the beach in the evening when the sun is down. I am writing this to show you how quickly life can turn on you and how you should always be grateful for what you have today because what you will have tomorrow is never guaranteed. A few months ago, I did not want to be alive, but now I am doing much better. Life is still hard, but I am so much happier.

CHAPTER TEN

LOVE

My liver GVHD seems to be improving every week, but it is still a very long process. My quality of life has been better as well. I go to the University of Miami Cancer Center twice a week for ECP, and the two other days of the week, I go to the University of Miami for physical therapy because of the avascular necrosis in my knees. Avascular Necrosis is so painful. My joints have been destroyed from treatment, and I need rehabilitation to make my knees stronger.

However, I find myself really enjoying the 30-minute drive to the hospital in the late mornings. I love putting on my favorite music, which consists of artists like Ian Dior, Dreamers, Girlfriends, and more. I have begun to drive to my appointments, but my mom still accompanies me because she loves me so much. The drives to the hospital are fun. I have found joy in driving; it makes me feel free, and after two years of not driving, it feels like a gift.

The one thing that these last few months have shown me is that you can still live life while immuno-suppressed. I have many restrictions, considering I am doing three treatments that all suppress my immune system. The Rezurock, which is a pill I take daily, the ECP that I do twice a week, and the immunotherapy called Eculizumab, which I do once every 4-5 weeks at Nicklaus Children's Hospital. My days when I am not going to the hospital consist of getting up late at around 11 a.m., working out, writing, making TikTok for cancer awareness, working on the podcast, talking to friends online, and going to the beach in the evening.

Surprisingly, there has been a good amount of socialization lately. I still follow very strict rules, but I am allowed to be around a few people I know well and trust. My good friend, Maximo, is a realtor in Miami Beach who still lives with his parents and has a great personality. We get along so well. I have known Maximo for a long time. We used to sail together when we were younger, and he was one of my friends who shaved his head while I was going through chemotherapy. We usually see each other once or twice a week, and it's very consistent. I would say he is my best friend, who is still in Miami. Maximo is tall, about 6'1, just like me, but he is tan, muscular, and charming. We talk about everything in life, but our main topic always ends up being girls. He always asks me how I have so much "sauce." "Sauce" is basically having game with girls. I always tell him I learned from being surrounded by beautiful nurses in the hospital 24/7, and this is actually true. My whole time at Nicklaus, I have been surrounded by the most beautiful, kind, and loving nurses. Fortunately, most of them are female and beautiful. That clearly helped my cancer journey and my attitude!

But lately, I have been on a hunt for a girl. I told Maxi that recently, my doctor said I could kiss girls. So, after two years of being in a hospital, suffering, and facing death, am I supposed to just get back out there like nothing has changed? Basically, it is a weird thing going back to the dating scene after cancer. I never thought I would ever be well enough to date anytime soon, but the time has come, and I have honestly been craving a meaningful, deep relationship with a woman. But unfortunately, it is not that simple. I am still in the hospital a few times a week, plus I live in Miami, and most girls' standard here is a guy who is able to go out and do fun stuff with them. So, I realized it was not going to be easy to find someone. I went on multiple dating apps, Bumble, Hindrance, Tinder, you name it. I had no success, but I was not worried. I know my self-worth and do not get caught up in little things like that. I just figured the right person would come into my life when it was time.

I was scrolling through TikTok one day when I saw a comment that caught my attention. It was from a girl I used to go to high school with. I realized she still lived in Miami. I decided to message her on TikTok and ask if she ever wanted to hang out. What is the worst that could happen? She says no? I am just looking for a friend and maybe a love interest. Who knows what could happen? She said yes to hanging out, and as usual, we went to the beach in the evening. The beach was my spot to hang out with people because it was outside, I did not have to wear a mask, and because it was the evening, I did not have to worry about the sun harming my fragile skin. It was perfect. We hung out, but we did not hit it off. We did not have a real connection, but I still found her attractive. She was nice. She was 5'1 with black hair, brown eyes, a nice fit body, and a pretty smile. The first time we hung out, I could not tell if she liked me, so I did not make a move. The second time we hung out, we did the same thing again: we went to the beach and talked. She likes to talk a lot, which is fine because it keeps the conversation going, but I could never really talk to her about anything deep. She seemed to have a barrier and did not understand my trauma or humor that well. Yet I still liked her. She was cute and sweet. She was a nice girl who hated the beach but would still come with me. When it was time for me to say bye to her, I debated going in for the kiss, but I did not want to make things awkward because she still did not give me any signs that she wanted me to, besides just laughing at my jokes. Then, a few days later, I texted her, and we hung out again. This time, we went to the beach, but it was different. It was more romantic; we went a little bit later, and the moon came out. We shared a towel and sat close but neither of us made a move until I was leaving the beach. Once we got to the beach exit, I decided it was now or never. I said jokingly, "What if we kissed at the public beach exit?"

I saw a little smile on her face, and she also looked a little nervous. But so was I. It had been so long since I kissed a girl. So many thoughts were running through my head. But she stared me in the eyes and said, "Sure." So I took the opportunity, and we kissed at the public beach exit. How funny. True story, though. I walked her to her building, hugged her goodbye, and drove home that evening feeling happy and accomplished. I blasted my favorite music on the drive home and texted her when I got home. Her response was a bit dry, as usual. I honestly expected her to be less dry and more excited, but she was not. I asked her for plans during the next week, but she was so busy that the next time we hung out was in 2 weeks, even though we only lived 20 minutes away from each other. I realized that even though we just kissed, she might not be right for me. I wanted someone who was really my soulmate, someone who understood me and my humor.

My days continued with ECP, physical therapy, and evening beach sessions with my mom. The next time this girl and I hung out, we kissed again, and it felt more passionate. Yet I have not seen her again since that day, and it has been over four weeks. She just tells me she is always busy, and she is not lying. She is a full-time student with a social life and a family. I understood that and respected her, but I was still sad. Even though we did not have a crazy connection, I am just happy I met someone. I would text her every few days to ask if she wanted to hang out, and she was always busy, so I stopped texting her and decided I needed to find someone who I had a real connection with and who was more open to my trauma, humor, and personality. She was great, but It was clearly not going to work. I realized that some things in life just aren't meant to be, and sometimes that's because there is something that fits you better out there. I knew there was someone out there who was actually my soulmate. So, instead of being discouraged, I kept looking. I knew the universe would help me.

One night, I was talking to one of my friends from High School named Bianca, who had been recently diagnosed with Ewing Sarcoma. I was the first person she told; not even her closest friends knew before me. But she told me she had cancer at a very dark time in my life when I was depressed, and my liver was nearly failing, so we never met up or really talked much after. But it had been nearly eight months since this happened, and I had been doing much better, so Bianca and I started to hang out. We would go to the beach, and she would come over sometimes. She and my mom got along really well. Bianca is beautiful, about 5'4, with a black wig, slim body, dark eyes, and a funny, dry sense of humor.

I was talking to Bianca, and she told me that her friend thought I was cute. I had no idea who her friend was, but I knew her from Instagram, so I decided to message Bianca's friend the next day. Her name was Suzie. She liked memes, and so did I. On one of her Instagram stories, she put a funny meme, and I responded to it. From there on, we started messaging each other on Instagram. Finally, I built up the courage to ask for her number, and we started texting. As we were texting, the conversation kept flowing super well. Suzie even asked me to hang out. I asked her if she was down to go to the beach on Monday at 6:30 pm. She said yes.

When Monday came around, I started to count down the hours until I was going to see her. I was so excited. I was also so nervous. I could feel my heart rate elevate and my body jitter at the idea of meeting up with this beautiful, funny, and kind girl I had been texting with. Suzie lived in South Beach, and I lived in North Miami. She was 30 minutes south of me. I used to live in South Beach when I was younger, but that was years ago, and it felt like it had been ages since I had been there. On the drive over, I was so nervous. I was blasting my music and trying not to think about it. Why was I nervous? I have been through cancer treatment and GVHD. What could possibly be worse than that? I do not know. But I was worried that I was not going to be enough. That Suzie was going to see that I was skinny, pale, and full of scars from treatment and think I was not attractive. I know I have my charm, but I still feel like a cancer patient to the rest of the world. I was anxious to see what a "normal" person thought of me.

When I finally arrived at her apartment, I texted her to come down and get in my car. She came down quickly, and there she was, with wild black hair, boots, beautiful legs, short shorts, and a nice top. She was gorgeous. It was a little awkward when she first got in the car, and we just had small talk. Yet once we arrived at the beach, it was different. There was a beautiful breeze, and the sun was setting. We shared my towel and sat close. We did not have a deep conversation like I had expected. Instead, we just made jokes and talked about our day-to-day lives, and there was not much conversation about cancer. Things got better once it got dark. We both found ourselves lying close next to each other, and Suzie wanted to play with my hair. She kept creeping closer to me in a romantic way, and for some reason, I felt frozen. The old me would have made a move instantly, but I decided to enjoy the intimacy. It was awkward but beautiful. She was running her hands through my hair while we were just staring at each other, talking nonsense and saying things because we were both too nervous to make a move. Finally, the tension became too much, and I told her I was going to fall asleep because her hands running through my hair was so relaxing. She said, "No, what can I do so you don't fall asleep?"

I said, "You can kiss me."

She said, "You have to kiss me".

And we did. Suzie was a phenomenal kisser, one of the best I had experienced in my life. The great thing about it was she was not weird about it. Right after we stopped kissing, she openly told me that I was a good kisser. This was such a great compliment to receive. It was the most different thing I have heard in over two years. The compliments I usually receive are about my cancer journey and strength, but to be complimented on something else felt so good and reassuring that I was still a human, not just a cancer patient. We kissed again, and then it was time for me to leave the beach, drop her off, and head home for dinner and medications. As I drove her home, we bonded over music, and I showed her my favorite songs. We were bonded. It felt like all the ice had been broken because of the kiss and that I was hanging out with someone I had known for years. She jammed to the music I played, and we laughed and smiled the whole way to her place. When I dropped her off, I went in for a short kiss, then she asked, "That's it?'" She wanted more, and I was very happy about that. We kissed for a little bit, and then we said our goodbyes. I drove home that night, blasting my music and feeling happy.

 I did not know what was to come next with us or if this would become a genuine relationship, but I had no other way to find out than to keep going and see what happened. I am always scared of getting emotionally invested in other people because it never seems to end well for some reason. I usually find myself falling in love with girls who are heartbreakers, and not in a good way. My issue is that I truly believe in love, and sometimes that can be so hard in this day and age, where we live in a hookup type of culture. But with my poor immune system and newly founded view on life, I am not searching for a hookup. I am searching for a real connection, something more than sex, something worthwhile. The next day, it was physical therapy for my knee, and then the next day, Wednesday, it was time for treatment, ECP again. I have really enjoyed ECP lately. Accessing my port is very painful because they use such giant needles to hook me up to the machine, but the nurses are so amazing. I find myself laughing with them, with Jesus, Sergio, and Carmen. Carmen and Sergio are both Hispanic, and Sergio often calls me "younger brother," and I have started to call him "younger brother" as well. We have grown very close, and I love them so much. They make the treatments worthwhile.

On Monday of this week, I met with my doctor. I drove to the hospital expecting to hear great news, in the hope that my ECP schedule would be reduced since my counts were looking good. I got to the hospital with my mom. We let the valet take our car, got into the hospital, and took the elevators to the third floor. I have not mentioned it yet, but the elevators at this hospital are super funky. They always take you to the wrong floor, and when we entered the elevator, my mom and I made some jokes with the nurses who were standing next to us about how the elevators "have a mind of their own."

Once my mom and I got to the third floor, we turned right and checked in. The lady who checks us in knows us well, but we never really talk to her. She always asks for my name, date of birth, and signature on the "hospital-based form." Once I sign the form, I get my white hospital wristband, and the lady asks me to make sure all the information is correct. "Of course," I say. The information is always correct. My mom and I left the crowded waiting area and went to the more isolated waiting area known as the "BMT waiting area." This area was made for BMT patients to wait in a more private setting because of their poor immunity post-transplant. After waiting for a little while, we went into the apheresis unit, and the phlebotomist, Lily, drew my labs. After Lily drew my labs, I was taken into the bed for ECP, and Sergio was my nurse. He accessed my port with the giant needles as usual, and we began treatment. Thirty minutes into the treatment, Dr. Wang and his Nurse practitioner arrived and started to talk to me.

Dr. Wang was very happy with my liver's improvement but still believed that I showed all the symptoms of Chronic GVHD and needed to continue this treatment for the next 3-6 months at the schedule of twice a week. This news was a little heartbreaking. I was really expecting something better. This meant I would not be traveling anytime soon or getting my vaccinations anytime soon. This meant more days in the hospital. There are 26 weeks in 6 months. With ECP being twice a week, this meant at least 52 more sessions of ECP. Fifty-two more times this year, I was going to have to get two giant needles shoved into my chest and have a bandage on me for 24 hours. However, I did not really process all of this until later that night when it was time to go to sleep, and I was really alone with my thoughts.

After treatment finished that day, I went home, worked on some stuff with my mom, and then went to Suzie's apartment. I was so nervous to go to her apartment; this usually meant sex. So before I went to her place, I went to CVS and bought condoms. I had actually never done this before, considering I was a virgin at the age of 21. It is a bit sad to admit this, but I have been isolated for the last two and a half years, so that did delay me a bit. Previous to my diagnosis, I just felt like I had never met the right person and that losing my virginity was something I needed to do with someone I genuinely loved. I bought a condom pack that said "sensitive" on it, thinking it was for sensitive skin, like mine, only to find out later that this meant "sensitive" as in feeling more during sex. I was a rookie in this field, so it made sense. Once I got the condoms, I texted a picture to my older, very experienced brother, and he told me that they should be good. I got into my red Hyundai Elantra, blasted my alternative/classic rock playlist, and was on my way. The drive was quicker than I expected, and as soon as I arrived, I realized I had nowhere to park because Suzie lived in a small apartment with no extra parking. So she told me to park in the back where I would not get towed. I managed to park in the back in a very tight spot. I got out of the car, and she welcomed me into her small apartment. It was exactly how I expected it to be. Suzie was an aspiring artist who worked at a bakery to make ends meet. She was also doing an apprenticeship at a tattoo shop in South Beach; she wanted to be a tattoo artist. Her house was full of posters, a small couch, and a bed that lay very low near her window. Upbeat music was playing, and it gave off a very chill vibe. I got to meet her beautiful yet scared cat named Scratch. I sat down next to her on her bed, and we started to talk. She told me to bring a Lego set to build, and I actually did. But as soon as I brought out the Lego set, I could tell she was not into it. She was joking about how complex it looked to build it with the pamphlet being so long, so instead, she just looked at me and kissed me. Before I knew it, she was on top of me, playing with my hair while we made out. My hands were gripping her thighs, and I could feel the passion. This was something I had longed for: the feeling of human touch and love. Suzie was very touchy, and she really seemed to know what she was doing. I felt embarrassed to know I was with such a beautiful and loving girl, and I was a virgin. I felt that if I told her while we were making out, this would turn her off, and she would distance herself from me. So I panicked, and after 10 minutes of just making out, I stopped kissing her and told her, "Hey, I had treatment today. I just don't have much of a sex drive. I'm sorry, I feel really bad." What I said was partially true.

She told me that she was actually on her period and that we could not have sex anyway. But we still kept making out, and we eventually took turns playing our favorite music on her speaker while we held each other closely, her hands wrapped in mine and her legs wrapped over my legs. We held hands and looked at each other. She was unlike any other girl I had talked to before; she liked the awkward, long eye contact, and intimacy was her thing. However, she had not really opened up to me yet. I had still not seen her emotional side besides her displays of affection for me. We are very similar yet also very different. She has the same sense of humor as me, which is why we bond so well, yet she does not have anywhere near the same medical trauma I have had in my life, or she has yet to open up about stuff like that. I was so used to people opening up to me quickly that I felt like I really had to work for this one. This was the affection I needed, though, the human contact I had desired for the last two years. I have been so isolated and trained to stay away from human contact that everything I was doing with this girl felt so refreshing. It was a feeling that I never wanted to leave my body. Yet after almost 2 hours of this, I had to leave to go home, take my medications, and sleep. I was exhausted from treatment and from the energy I spent while making out with this girl. I felt a little embarrassed when I left because I knew I did not tell her I was a virgin, and I am sure she expects me not to be one. I had never had an issue getting girls in my life. It was just the trust thing I had an issue with. I was funny, confident, and decent-looking my whole life. No one would guess I was a virgin, but it was a secret that I knew, and I was so embarrassed by it. Yet I knew I needed to tell Suzie this eventually because she would find out one way or another the next time I went over.

I got home that night, ate my favorite meal, Chick-fil-A, and then went to bed. Once I went to bed, a weird feeling crept upon me. I had a feeling of sadness, even though today was a great day. It was a feeling that I had not felt in a while. I was sad about the treatment. I knew that with my continuing ECP for the next six months. I would not be able to go out, and I would not be able to go back to school or do anything really besides what I have been doing. It also made me feel bad about Suzie because I really like this girl, and if things move forward with us, I feel it would be unfair for her not to go out just to be with me. If she were to become my girlfriend, I would be putting a burden on her because I would not be able to go out with her. She lives a more normal life of a 20-year-old girl in Miami. She has friends and does stuff that people with a functioning immune system do. I was scared of what would happen between us because of my health.

As I began to worry about catching feelings and having my heart broken, I remembered something. It was October 27th, 2022, which is the two-year anniversary of my bone marrow transplant. It was a huge day, and on my drive to physical therapy, I felt happy about this, but on the way home, I received a text that would derail my celebration and put me into a feeling of survivor's guilt. I was driving home from physical therapy when I stopped at a red light and saw my phone light up. It was a text from Najla, who is a friend of mine going through cancer treatment for her rare sarcoma. The text read, "I am starting hospice care, the chemo isn't working, and it's too late for immunotherapy. I have a few weeks left." I was heartbroken and brought to tears on the way home. The music I was listening to suddenly became background noise, and I felt my mind go blank. I was shocked. Najla had just told me a few weeks ago that her chemo was working. I really thought she was going to survive. I was destroyed. I loved Najla. We made TikToks together, and I had the world's biggest crush on her before I met Suzie. I used to fantasize about Najla and I becoming super close. She was an athlete like me before she had cancer, a synchronized swimmer. She was 5,11 with blue eyes and blonde hair. She was gorgeous, funny and had so much to live for. She was a student at the University of Florida, and everyone loved her. She was known for her funny TikToks, and I was honored to meet her and be her friend. While I was treated at the adult cancer center at Sylvester, she was being treated at the pediatric center across the street because she was 18 years old. I feel so guilty today. How did I survive two years post-transplant, and Najla is not going to make it? I was devastated. Her cancer was once in remission, but it came back, and this time, it was too aggressive and rapidly growing.

I am honestly sad to say this, but learning of this has taught me so much. You never know if you have tomorrow. I sometimes let my ego get in the way of things and even take life for granted. I guard my heart because I am afraid of getting hurt, but in the end, we all suffer either way. I suffer because I protect myself from getting hurt, but I realized today, with this news, that it is better to give someone your heart than not to. It's better to give love a try and see what happens. Life is so short, and it can turn around in an instant. So why do we try so hard to protect our hearts? Why are we so afraid of love? What is it that makes us this way? Before I was diagnosed with cancer, I had my heart broken multiple times, but I realized that every time, it was by someone I did not truly love. So now I must love and learn to show love because, after all I have been through, love is all I have.

I continued my schedule of going to the hospital four times a week, but this week was different. On Friday, I led my support group as usual, but I headed over to Suzie's apartment once I was finished with my group. I was nervous. I felt that this was going to be the day we had sex. I stopped at CVS and bought some condoms, walking around looking like someone with experience when, in fact, it was quite the opposite. Once I bought the condoms, I drove over to Suzie's apartment. I was nearly shaking at arrival for some reason, but when I got inside, I was not nervous. She was so laid back, chill, and understanding. We got close to each other in her bed and started cuddling. She was tired like me, and we just seemed to understand each other, but one thing led to the next, and before I knew it, I found myself admitting to her that I was a virgin. She was completely understanding, and we had sex. Afterwards, I wondered why I waited so long. Yes, it was good, but it was not perfect. It was not even scary or something I should have ever been worried about. After we had sex, we laid next to each other, and it was super nice. We listened to music and chilled. Then, I was on my way home. The whole weekend, I sat at home, questioning what would come of this relationship with Suzie. Would we end up boyfriend and girlfriend? Or would we end up in some sort of situationship?

Then Monday came. It was a busy day. That morning, I got up and went to Nicklaus Children's Hospital. I was having my 2-year post-bone marrow transplant tests. The morning started off with a Pulmonary Function test—one of my least favorite tests. I had to sit inside a little glass box and blow my lungs out into a machine. This test aimed to better understand my lung capacity and see how my lungs are functioning. The test is actually quite difficult, and Bill, the tech in charge of this test, was super kind. He explained it to me super well and was very understanding of my struggles during the test. After the PFT was finished, he told me that it was the best I had ever done. I was so proud. After the PFT, I had an Echo of my heart and then immunotherapy. The day was long, but finally, I got home at around 4:30. Once I got home, I realized I had made plans to see Suzie again that day. So, after the hospital, I drove to South Beach to see her, and we cuddled and held each other close. We were both exhausted. She was exhausted from her long day at work. I was exhausted from my day at the hospital, and we just held each other. It was one of the most peaceful and beautiful moments in my life—to be held by someone that you care about so much and have that love reciprocated. It was a moment I did not want to end. I had never felt this with someone before, never have I ever had a girl I liked hold me like this. It was heartwarming and made me feel like everything was going to be alright despite all of my health issues.

The next day, I was back to ECP as usual, with two giant needles in my chest, hours in the hospital, then home. The next day, the hospital again. I got Covid antibodies and then had physical therapy. The next day, I met with an orthopedic surgeon. It was Thursday, November 3rd, 2022. I went into this appointment expecting the surgeon to say I needed an elbow replacement. My elbow had been hurting for a while, and it turned out that the same necrosis I have in my knee is also in my elbow. But at this appointment, I got awful news. The surgeon said he had never seen an elbow like this before and that the necrosis in my elbow would only be fixed by a surgery that is not even performed in the United States anymore. I needed a distal humerus replacement, but this was not an FDA-approved procedure anymore. He also told me I should not be lifting any weights at all. This was devastating news. I was once again heartbroken. Life was great because of Suzie and because of the fact I was doing treatment outpatient now, but things were still not perfect—not even close. I wished for some normalcy. I wished my body would just be how it used to be. I could not work out anymore. Just a few months ago, I was working out almost every day. Now I was struggling to lift 5lbs. It was such a shock that there was no fix. It was devastating to hear. I would never return to the person I once was physically. Every time I tried to do some type of weight bearing, my elbows throbbed in pain. I was sad, but at this point, I had gotten used to these types of disappointment. At the end of the day, I am still alive, and that is enough. If I can't work out, that is okay. I am still here and breathing.

I went to ECP the next day and was in a better mood. The treatment went well, and as usual, my nurses were super funny and lifted my spirits. Jesus, Carmen, and Sergio had become part of my family. Once I went home from treatment, I had my support group, and then I went to see Suzie. I went over, and we watched a movie. We cuddled the whole time. We watched "Revenge of the Sith," one of my favorite Star Wars movies of all time. Then, after the movie, we had our routine time in the bedroom. She walked me to my car as I was leaving, and we held hands on the way there. I kissed her goodbye and drove home. I went home that night and realized something. I really liked this girl. I mean, I REALLY liked her. There was a real connection between us. I drove the 30 minutes home, and all I could think about was her and how she was changing my life one day at a time. We had made plans to go play pool the next day in an uncrowded bar because of my poor immune system. I was excited.

The next day came and it was Saturday night. I drove to South Beach to pick Suzie up from work, and then we went to play pool. It was my first time going out in over two and a half years. This was my first time leaving the house past 10 pm to go somewhere besides the emergency room. It was a surreal feeling. I felt out of rhythm. I threw on my skinny jeans, my black shirt, my Nikes, and a chain. I felt fresh and a little bit like my old self. I picked up Suzie from her work, and then Suzie and I drove to South Beach, where her friend Jess lives (Suzie had been crashing at Jess's place because she recently left her apartment due to a bad relationship with her roommate) and we walked over to a small bar on 2nd street. The bar was loud and full of football fans raving at the current college football game going on. To the corner of the bar was a small empty space with a pool table. There was no one playing pool, and I was isolated from the rest of the people in the bar. My weak immune system was able to exhale after seeing how uncrowded this part of the bar was. It was so refreshing to be out doing something social with someone. Suzie and I played two games of pool, and I lost both. But I did not care. We laughed the whole time and had so much fun together.

After those two games, we walked back to Jess's apartment, cuddled, and talked. Then, after a while, we both sat outside on Jess's porch under the stars and began to talk. Suzie said to me, " I have to tell you something. I do not want to see anyone else besides you. I hope the feeling is mutual….."

Of course, the feeling was mutual. I told her that. We had an extremely deep conversation; one thing led to another, and I ended up telling Suzie my deepest and most personal secret. I told her I had once tried to kill myself a little over eight months ago. It was hard to open up, but I always felt that being open was key for things to stay healthy in a relationship between people. She also ended up telling me about some trauma of her own. This whole time we were talking, we were holding hands, sitting right next to each other outside at 1 am in South Beach under the beautiful dark sky. It was majestic, and I realized I wanted Suzie to be my girlfriend. She kept asking me if I had a question to ask her. I knew she wanted me to ask her to be my girlfriend, so I joked around with her a little bit and tried to play dumb to see how she reacted. After a few minutes of doing this, I stopped playing around and realized I needed to ask her the question. I did, and she said yes. She was my first real girlfriend. Then and there, it really hit me. Eight months ago, my liver was failing, and I tried to end my own life. I was miserable and had no hope. Yet here I was eight months later, leading a cancer support group, living my best immunocompromised life, having a girlfriend, and being happy. Being in love was a weird feeling. But it was all I wanted. Suzie even asked me if there was a place I would want to go once I was done with ECP, and I honestly could not think of an answer because the only place I wanted to be was right here and now, with this girl holding hands talking in the middle of the night. At around 1:40 am, she walked me to my car, and we held hands. Once we got to my car, we started staring at the stars and could not stop. After a few minutes, we began to say goodbye, and then I said, "Hey, I should drop you off so you don't have to walk home alone at night." She agreed. Suzie usually worked late, lived 30 minutes away from me, and did not drive. She usually walked home alone at night. She usually texts me when she is walking because I can tell she does not feel safe, so I found much comfort in knowing I was able to drive her home that night and she was safe. We kissed goodbye, and I was on my way home. I drove home the whole way excited and full of joy, knowing I had a girlfriend.

Life was changing. I found myself realizing that for years before cancer, I had been scared of doing certain things and truly being myself. Yet it took a whole cancer diagnosis and years of treatment to make me realize who I am.

Lately, I found myself listening to throwback music at night and waiting for my tiredness to kick in so I could fall asleep. It has been odd lately. So much good had happened: I laughed a lot, I had sex, and I had a girlfriend, but I still felt somewhat lost. I still long for health. I still long for the healthy joints I used to have. I still long for the early morning surf sessions I used to have. I miss the ocean, the gym, and my friends. I felt a bit lonely, even though I was surrounded by love. Every night, my skin itches, and I wake up in the middle of the night. I am stuck with the same food every day. It just feels like life is on repeat. It is also killing me slowly, knowing I will never go back to the person I was. Knowing that I am walking around half the person I was before cancer, physically, that is. I also know I have to go back to school at some point, and I am going to be a freshman in college. I just felt like I was restarting, like I was given a second chance, but at a harder life.

To make things harder, Najla passed away. She had texted me when she was in hospice, and I was supposed to meet her before she was gone. But that never happened. After about a week in hospice, she stopped answering my texts, and I knew it was over. I messaged her sister on Instagram and found out that Najla was in a coma/ unresponsive state. A few days later, I heard that he had passed away. I was absolutely heartbroken and destroyed. On Thursday, November 17th, 2022, she died. That day, I was so sad. I texted my girlfriend Suzie and made plans to see her the next evening.

On Friday evening, I went to see Suzie. I picked her up, and when we got out of the car. I hugged her, kissed her on the forehead, and told her how much I appreciated her. It was the moment that Najla passed away that refreshed my perspective on life and made me remember to always appreciate the ones around me. Suzie was changing my life and becoming the beginning of a new era in my time. She was showing me things no one had ever shown me before. She genuinely seemed to appreciate me and was honest about everything. That night, we went to a bar and played pool with Bianca, who was her friend who set us up. After playing pool, Suzie, Bianca, and I walked back to the apartment and put on some Netflix. Bianca and her other friend, Jessica, were preparing to go out that night. But Suzie knew I could not go out, so we chilled at Jess's. Already going to an uncrowded bar was a stretch with my poor, damaged immune system.

Yet that night with Suzie felt magical. We watched my favorite show from my early High school years: "Trailer Park Boys." Then we just cuddled on the bed and held each other for hours. We had deep conversations, long kissing, tons of intimacy, and a lot of passion. At that moment, I realized I could find myself falling in love with this girl. She was the perfect mixture of socially awkward, funny, cute, and deep. She had an edge to her on the outside that was not matched by the sweet, innocent girl on the inside. She dressed in all black with a very strong look that came off as intimidating, but she was soft on the inside. Just like most of us, Suzie was lost as well. She explained to me that she felt she was going backward in life. She recently moved out of her apartment and had been working the same job for the last two years. She had to move in with her friend Jess and stop her Tattoo apprenticeship. That night, she did not want me to leave. We were so deep in each other's arms that it felt as if we were one. But I had to go home and take my medications; it was needed. But before we left, she asked me if I had ever been in love. I answered, "No, have you?"

She said, "No." But it was an awkward answer because we both felt the tension between us and knew that part of us wanted to say yes, but it was too early in the relationship to say so. The truth was when she asked me, I wanted to say, "I have not, but I have a feeling I soon will be."

I drove home that night with a feeling in my chest that I had never felt before. I felt very comfortable with Suzie and felt a deep connection with her. Every time I saw her, I liked her more and more.

That entire weekend I felt like shit. I think I caught something. I had a migraine, a lack of appetite, and was exhausted. I found out that Monday was Najla's service.

Monday came, and thankfully, I was feeling better. My mom and I drove an hour to Boca Raton and made it to the service. The service was beautiful. We arrived, and immediately, I felt it all. I met Najla's grandmother, sister, uncle, mom, and some of her friends. At that moment, it felt all so real looking at her casket with the beautiful flowers surrounding it. There were tables spread around three different rooms, each filled with people that Najla knew and affected. Each room was filled with people who had lost someone important in their lives to a terrible disease known as cancer. I watched as her father greeted tons of people, shook their hands, and was told they were sorry for his loss. When my father passed away, we did not have a large service like this, so it felt strange to me. But it also made it feel so real. It was so sad. Her little sister was 16, now without an older sister to help guide her in life. Her dad was now without her TikTok partner. Najla and her dad were famous for making funny videos together; they connected like my mom and I did. They were bonded, and now they are separated. I felt the survivors' guilt heavy. Why did treatment work for me and not for her?

On the drive home from the service, I could not choose what music to play, so I played my sad music and cried listening to a song that said, "This world was too painful. I hope it's better where you are". These lyrics were so relevant to Najla. I was devastated. The girl I once had a crush on and was so happy to be friends with would never be able to talk to me again. I will never be able to Facetime her, make another TikTok with her, or see her again.

She was really gone. It all hit me on that drive home. I remember so clearly the first time she messaged me on Instagram, and then we started talking and making plans to go surf when we were both done with treatment. But now that will never happen. Her family has to spend Thanksgiving and Christmas without Najla. It is no doubt going to be a hard holiday season.

The days dragged on, and I continued my schedule of ECP twice a week and physical therapy twice a week. I found myself sad, however. I was finally in a relationship, and I really liked the girl, but all I wanted was for time to pass. I just wanted to be done with ECP and PT and be able to go back to normal life. But it made me realize that I will never go back to normal life. It was a sad moment of realization. I had Chronic GVHD, which meant I would be in treatment for the next several years, if not for life. It was not up to me to decide what would happen with my health; it was up to the universe, and learning to let go of control was such a hard thing to do. I enjoyed the days at ECP and PT because they gave me purpose and made me feel like I had something I was obligated to do. But I soon received news that I was reaching a Plateau in PT, and the same was happening with ECP. Without a knee replacement, I could not really make any more progress in PT, and the ECP had kind of reached its maximum effect for my GVHD. I received both of these news in the same week, and it was a bit sad. I was going to discontinue PT, just plain and simple, but ECP was going to be continued, just at a lesser rate. I was still going to do it. It was just going to change to twice a week every other week.

Yet, my relationship with Suzie began to blossom. I found myself finally in love, for real. We hung out on the day before Thanksgiving, and she told me she loved me. I looked her right in the eyes, held her hand, and told her I loved her too. I felt it in the sex as well. It was much more passionate, and when we would hang out on the weekends and sometimes during my busy week, we would often find each other holding hands while walking, cuddling in bed, and sharing more intimate moments. It became increasingly obvious to me that I had my insecurities as the relationship went on. I found myself so scared of what would happen if I relapsed or if Suzie would leave me because my health issues made it so that I could not do everything socially with her. She is young and in great physical shape. I am young as well, but quite the opposite. My joints, bones, and immune system were in horrible shape, and I felt like a burden in the relationship sometimes. But I keep telling myself that my benefits outweigh my health issues.

The hardest part about everything I have been dealing with the last few months has been the pain. My knees ache when I walk more than a mile, and my elbow cannot lift weights anymore. I have lost my outlet for my anger and frustration. I used to work out to let anger and frustration out, but now I cannot. So, I have moved on to the next chapter of my life: acceptance.

Accepting the fact that after an illness like cancer, you may never return to who you were before. Accepting that is okay. Accepting that you have trauma and you may never get over it, but you find ways to cope with it and live with what happened. Accepting that this is not the life you dreamed of but the life you were given. Lastly, accepting love and being able to allow good things in your life because you deserve them. We often receive good things and believe they are too good to be true, and we try to sabotage them because we cannot see ourselves as deserving. But the truth is we are all deserving, and we have all been through too much to deny love or kindness. We need love. We are humans, and as social creatures, love is what gets us through tough times. Love is what is getting me through this tough time in my life.

Love will get you through the hardest times in your life, but some people are not surrounded by that love. Some people will have to face their challenges alone. Whether we like it or not, we do most of the hard things we have to do in life alone. Almost all of the suffering I have endured has been alone. I was the one who got all the treatment and went through all the pain, yet there were people by my side who cheered me along every step of the way. The cheering and the love help so much, but it does not change what you are dealing with. In life, if we want to get through any tough time, we have to be resilient and strong but also vulnerable.

As time went on into the new year of 2023, my liver began to act up again. I was doing ECP twice a week every other week, but this was moved back to every week twice a week. The GVHD doctor believed that the reduction of ECP caused the liver to flare up and that putting me back to ECP twice a week would help with this. Yet, it has become so draining. ECP twice a week meant more time in the hospital, more needles in my port, and more pain. Yet it was my only choice if I wanted to survive, so I continued on. I found myself picking up the guitar instead of working out because my avascular necrosis had gotten so bad. The days sort of all feel the same; either I am in the hospital or doing something cancer-related. But ECP, my treatment for GVHD twice a week, felt just as tiring. The needles in my chest, the fun nurses who laugh and joke with my mom and me the whole, the blood coming out of my body through 2 separate lines entering a machine and then returning to me, however, gets quite old fast. Don't get me wrong, I love my nurses, and I am thankful to be alive, but knowing that there is no real goal for me with this treatment besides staying alive can be hard. Most cancer patients get an end date to treatment, a bell to ring, and a celebration, and then their restrictions are lifted. But Chronic GVHD patients don't know such royalties. We are the survivors of cancer who went through a transplant only to get hit with another incurable disease.

However, things in my day-to-day life besides my illness were going well. I still have ECP twice a week, but I have accepted my disease, and I understand why this happened to me.

I found myself picking up the guitar. My mom had an acoustic guitar, and I took some lessons with it at a place near our apartment. I was hooked. The guitar was my new favorite thing. I could not surf or work out, but I found a new outlet: music. I was so happy with it that after a month, I bought my own electric guitar and started playing rock and metal songs. This was my favorite type of music, and it filled my soul.

On the other hand, my mom and I started speaking, we started a podcast, and we are now trying to spread our message of love and hope to the entire world. We have spoken at a few events and hope to speak at many more. We advocate for cancer awareness, lead support groups, and do our best to help people. It has been our purpose, and I am glad I went through all of this awful stuff because it has given me a reason to keep going. The podcast, the speaking events, the support groups, and our presence on social media were our "why." I feel so fulfilled these days because what I am doing is good work, and it helps not only others but also me.

I have a beautiful and kind mother, a great family, a wonderful medical team and a perfect group of friends. Despite everything I go through on a daily basis with Chronic GVHD, I choose to look at the good because that is the best way to live life. I still have my struggles and my bad days of course, but I chose to accept it and realize I cannot change it, so why worry so much? I realized that life is just about living, and as long as I am doing that, I will continue on and do my best. There is still much ahead of me in this life, and I look forward to it. I wonder what the universe will have planned for me next.

CONCLUSION

MY MESSAGE TO YOU

There are many things I want you to take away from my story, but first off, I want you to understand that getting out of your comfort zone is the best thing you can do for yourself. If you really want to grow, do not wait until it is too late in life to do so. Do not wait until you are too old to do the things you wish you could have done. Live your life every day knowing you will not have regrets when you die. I think so much about my life would be different if I did not get cancer, and I realize that cancer has put my life into perspective. It sucks, but it made me who I am today.

If I could have become healthy after my transplant instead of living with a chronic illness known as Chronic GVHD, I would have traveled the world. If, in the future, I do get better and my immune system improves, I will find a way to travel and see the things I have dreamt of. Life is short. Please tell everyone that you love, that you love them. Get out of your comfort zone, try a new hobby, try a new job, follow your dreams, and travel the world while you are healthy. When I was cooped up in the hospital, I would have done anything to get out. So, to all of you who are out of the hospital and reading this, please take a moment to appreciate your health and what you have. There is so much life has to offer. Do not wait until it is taken away from you to appreciate it. I would kill to be able to go on another surf trip, but I can't. So take advantage of what you have because it is precious.

NOTHING IN LIFE IS LINEAR

We often think that things will go linear and we will consistently improve or get better at something, but that is not the case. Things go up and down all the time. That includes healing. Take my story, for example. I was so ready to get through the Bone marrow transplant process and be back to surfing. To this day, I am not surfing. Yet I am still here and healing. Things in life are slow, so be easy on yourself.

You have to be patient and think of it like you are driving a car somewhere, and then there is a bridge you have to cross. But that bridge goes up, and you have to stop for a while and wait. Instead of going back to your old ways, turning around, and looking for a different route, wait for the bridge to come down and continue going. You will constantly face traffic jams and red lights in life, but the thing is, you have to keep driving. Even when it seems like you might be stuck in traffic forever, just know it will eventually clear up and that before you know it, you will be driving smoothly again.

After my transplant, my mom and I made a video of us dancing for Instagram, doing the "cha cha." We did this dance because we were constantly going forward and then back. Things were constantly two steps forward and 1 step back. That is how you have to take your healing and the progress you make in life, whether it be in your job, your love life, or your mental health. Nothing is going to come easy, and if it does, it doesn't feel rewarding. So take your time and be patient with yourself. Life is not a marathon; life is simply about living and finding ways to be content and present.

To this day, I still do ECP and take immunosuppressants. I could possibly be taking immunosuppressants for the rest of my life, so that means no sun, a difficult time traveling, poor immunity, and a packed hospital schedule. Yet the thing is, I am slowly improving, not just physically but also mentally. Healing from trauma takes time. After I tried to end my life, I would get flashbacks every single day and have to break down crying, talking to my Mom or my therapist about how I felt. But after a few months, it started to get better, and the more I talked about what happened, the more I accepted it instead of trying to forget about it, and that is the biggest issue with trauma: we try to forget it instead of trying to help heal it and understand how it affects us.

I can openly talk about trying to end my life now because I understand why it happened. My advice to you, the reader of this book, is to find a way to comprehend your trauma instead of hiding it. Express it through writing, crying, screaming, or talking. Once we release it from our system, we can begin to heal gradually. But don't rush yourself, and remember, patience is key. Feeling broken is normal sometimes, but things will improve as time goes by.

LOVE

Love is why I am still here. If you are reading this and you have love in your life, just know anything is possible. The reason I survived is because of the love in my life. Love is healing, love is a connection, and it is key in dark times. Having someone you love near your side can turn things around when things go wrong.

My mom was my savior so many times, and so were my nurses in the hospital. The people around me are the reason why I am who I am. When I was depressed, it was the people around me who saved me; it was not just myself. I am so lucky to have had all the love in my life.

I should dedicate a whole book just to my mom, Ashlee Cramer. She literally never left my side once during everything. I may not have written that much about her during my story, but that was because I was focused on just telling the story. My Mom is an angel sent down from heaven. She saved my life multiple times and is the reason I wrote this book. She is my best friend and also can be a nurse and a therapist by now with everything I put her through.

GRATITUDE

If you are healthy, please take advantage of that. As a 22-year-old who can barely lift any weights anymore because of avascular necrosis or work a real job because of my health, I am telling you to please be grateful for what you have. I have avascular necrosis in my elbows, shoulders, knees, and total body. I have pain almost every day of my life. I cannot get any sun, my lung function is only 69%, and my heart seems to have a small complication as well. Things are hard. I wish I could just travel somewhere, get a random job, and explore the world. But I cannot. So that is why I am encouraging those of you who are healthy to go and live your life while you can. I do not mean to scare you, but you can die any day or get cancer any day. So, what is really holding you back from being who you want to be?

Of course, I know it is hard to actually chase your dreams and do everything you want to do if I am being realistic, but still, it does not mean you can't. But the most important thing I want to stress to you is simple. It's called gratitude. Be grateful for the small things in life, and when you feel like you don't have enough, go and count everything you do have in your life, and you will see you probably have enough. Living is simple, but we overcomplicate things and constantly compare ourselves to others. Enjoy being yourself and be grateful for who you are.

No two people are the same, so make sure to love yourself. You live with yourself, so why not be kind?

MY FATHER

I lost my father to cancer when I was 14. My mom had to work so hard for us three kids, and she gave us a dream life. When I was diagnosed with cancer, the world turned upside down, and all I could think of was my dad. He passed away when I was so young, but he taught me so much.

Losing my father at a young age taught me to be grateful for the time you spend with people because you never really know when the last day you will see them will be. My father was one of the reasons I pushed through everything and kept going on. I knew I had to do this for him.

It is really crazy to think about it: my father passed away from cancer, I got cancer, my father needed a bone marrow transplant, I got a bone marrow transplant, my father had depression, and I went through depression. It almost feels like, in a way, I am my father—just a younger version. After all, I am playing the guitar now. My father used to play guitar, and he was a very successful sound engineer in France. I am so proud of my father, and I hope he is proud of me, too. It is crazy how alike we are. They do say we turn into our parents for a reason.

ACCEPTANCE AND ADAPTING

Do not be a victim of your situation. You have more control than you think.

I thought that because I had avascular necrosis, osteoporosis, and GVHD, I would not be able to work out. But the truth is I have found ways around it. Instead of being sad because I could not work out like I used to, I adapted and found new ways to work out. I can't use weights over 7 pounds, but I am still able to use weights. I choose to look at what I can do, not what I can't. That is one of the most important lessons I have learned. That idea of living life by focusing on what you can do and not what you can't will radically change your life. It will improve it drastically because you will be so much more grateful for everything. I am often amazed that I have vision, can walk, and can breathe. You should always remember that gratitude is one of the keys to living a full and happy life.

I had to adapt so many times in my journey, and I still do so every day. Adapting is key in life and key in tough times. So is acceptance. If you can accept your situation, you can adapt to it. Life is hard, but we can make it through the toughest times by accepting our situation. I had to accept the fact that I had cancer before I could get through it. I have accepted the fact that I have a chronic illness, and life will have its challenges. No matter what you are going through, you can get through it. You have the strength. Just remember to trust in yourself and take your time.

CONNECTION

Connection is key, I like to say. Throughout my whole journey, my mom was by my side. She is the sole reason I am still alive to this day. She taught me that if you can be by somebody's side in their toughest times, it could save their life. My friends and all the support I had are the reasons I was able to stay positive in my darkest moments. Even when I gave up and tried to end my life, the support lifted me up once again.

I remember when I lost my hair at the beginning of my chemotherapy treatment, all my friends shaved their heads in unison with me. It was one of the most beautiful things I had ever witnessed in my life. My friends showed me that I was not alone. That they would be there by my side through thick and thin. That made me so happy. If you are going through a tough time, find someone who has been through something similar. If you can't relate to your friends because they have not been through what you have been through, then find someone who has. There are plenty of options online for support. There are so many apps that offer free support groups. Seriously, don't ever feel alone because your friends or family cannot understand your problems. There are many people out there who will understand your problems. You just have to find them, and sometimes finding them takes time. Be patient, and just know you are truly not alone. You are not crazy for needing support. When I was depressed, I thought I was crazy, but it was normal, and it made sense why I was so depressed. It happens; it's life, and thankfully, there is help out there.

When I was in the hospital for my last admission, I met Alex. He was amazing. He was one of the reasons I kept going after my episode of depression. We would meet at the end of the hallway in the hospital by a huge glass window and watch the sunset every night. It was our tradition. Alex and I would talk about everything, and he made me feel normal because he was someone near my age in the hospital that could relate to some of my struggles.

Going through a time in your life when you feel isolated from others is hard. It is nearly impossible to get through something like cancer without a caregiver, and I truly believe it is the same for any struggles, whether it be anxiety, anorexia, or cancer; we all need someone to connect with who can make us feel normal and not so isolated.

That's why I talk to cancer patients, and I have my own set of "cancer friends" because we understand each other in ways that our "healthy friends" could never. But I still keep my "healthy friends" because you cannot merely make your whole life about your illness or your struggles. Sometimes, you need to decompress and do something that makes you feel normal or healthy.

Connection is key, but time alone is also good for us. When we are alone, we stop learning so much about how to be with others, and we learn to be with ourselves. When we are up late at night, unable to sleep because our thoughts are running wild, sometimes that is where we find ourselves. Almost every night before I fall asleep, I check in with myself and make sure that I am okay. Being alone is a power, but only being able to be alone is a problem, and the same goes for being too social. We need to find the balance, the perfect mixture of alone time and time with others, to truly understand who we are.

But remember, just because you feel alone doesn't mean you are. There are people out there who would be willing to be your friend. You just might not have found them yet, and if you did, make sure to keep them. Life is too short not to be around the ones you love the most.

DON'T BE AFRAID OF AGING

My grandmother is 82, and she is still the epitome of health; my mom is in her 50s. Yet they both work out every day. Health is wealth, and that is a fact. I realized that getting old is a blessing. It means you have lived a long life and learned so much. Aging is scary, but so is getting cancer at a young age and wondering if you will get the chance to age because not everyone does. Getting old is beautiful. I am only 22, but if I get to live a long life and become gray-haired and wrinkly, I will be so happy.

If my story has taught me anything, it's that you have to be present and grateful for all you have in life because you never know when it can all vanish.

Thank you for reading. I love you, and you are more loved than you think.

AFTERWORD

I should dedicate a whole book just to my mom, Ashlee Cramer. She literally never left my side once during everything I went through, I should probably rephrase that and say "everything we went through". I may not have written that much about her during my story, but that was because I was focused on just telling it. My Mom is literally an angel sent down from heaven. She saved my life multiple times and is the sole reason I wrote this book. She is my best friend, she can be a nurse and a therapist by now with everything I put her through.

In the Bone marrow transplant unit while I was sick and hallucinating my mom cleaned up my vomit, helped me shower, helped me walk and ordered me food when I was too weak to do any of it. My Mom as a caregiver did all the dirty work and did not get enough credit. People think I am strong, but I am nothing without my Mother by my side. My Mom is the reason I am who I am to this day. She held my hand when I was very sick and let me cry in her arms. She was with me through every minute of my journey. She handled all the insurance issues, she drove me to the hospital every day, she slept by my side every single night in the hospital. Not once did my Mom leave me when I was admitted for 5 months. She helped talk me through everything I went through and she gave me the courage to survive and keep going. My Mom, Ashlee is a wonder and she really is an angel sent down from the Heavens. She is the funniest, smartest person I know.

The truth is, she is the reason I got out of my major depression. Yes, other people helped but she was the one by my side every single day. I love you so much Mom. I am sorry to have put you through so much, but I am grateful you never gave up on me. My brother Steven and my sister Jennifer were amazing and they still are. They never gave up on me either. When I was admitted to the hospital, my brother came almost every single day to see my Mom and I. My brother would go on daily walks with my mom and I in the hospital and sit in our hospital room and build legos with my mom and I.

My sister tried to visit, but she was under 18 and the rules at the time in the hospital only allowed 2 adults and one patient per room., which were my Mom and brother. My sister snuck in a few times, but we would FaceTime with her all the time. My siblings are a blessing and they are a huge part of my journey and a big reason why I am still here. When I was home, being with my brother and sister was one of the biggest things I looked forward to. I love them so much. My Grandmother and her boyfriend Mack showed my mom and I much love and would visit us when we were home.

On the days where My Mom and I felt good enough we would drive up to my Grandmother's place and we would see her and her boyfriend Mack. Mack was more than just my Grandma's boyfriend, he was basically my Grandfather and felt like a father figure to my Mom and I. I am so blessed that I have been surrounded by so much love throughout everything. To my Mom, Steven, Jennifer, Grandma, Mack and everyone else who has shown me love, thank you so much. I love you. You are the reason I am here.

Printed in Great Britain
by Amazon